Knight's Cross and Oak-Leaves Recipients 1939–40

Gordon Williamson · Illustrated by Ramiro Bujeiro

First published in Great Britain in 2004 by Osprey Publishing
Elms Court, Chapel Way, Botley, Oxford OX2 9LP, United Kingdom.
Email: **info@ospreypublishing.com**

ISBN 1 84176 641 0

Editorial by Ilios Publishing, Oxford, UK (www.iliospublishing.com)
Design: Alan Hamp
Index: Alison Worthington
Originated by The Electronic Page Company, Cwmbran, UK
Printed in China through World Print Ltd.

04 05 06 07 08   10 9 8 7 6 5 4 3 2 1

A CIP catalogue record for this book is available from the British Library.

FOR A CATALOGUE OF ALL BOOKS PUBLISHED BY
OSPREY MILITARY AND AVIATION PLEASE CONTACT:

Osprey Direct UK
P.O. Box 140, Wellingborough, Northants, NN8 2FA, UK
E-mail: **info@ospreydirect.co.uk**

Osprey Direct USA
c/o MBI Publishing, P.O. Box 1, 729 Prospect Ave
Osceola, WI 54020, USA
E-mail: **info@ospreydirectusa.com**

www.ospreypublishing.com

Artist's note

The original paintings from which the colour plates in this book were prepared are available for private sale. All reproduction copyright whatsoever is retained by the Publishers. All enquiries should be addressed to the illustrator.

Ramiro Bujeiro, C.C.28, 1602 Florida, Argentina

The Publishers regret that they can enter into no correspondence upon this matter.

Linear measurements

Measurements in this volume are provided in metric units.
A conversion table is provided below.

1 millimetre (mm)	0.0394 in.
1 centimetre (cm)	0.3937 in.
1 metre (m)	1.0936 yards
1 kilometre (km)	0.6214 miles
1 kilogram (kg)	2.2046 lb
1 tonne (t)	0.9842 long ton (UK)

Photographic credits

Unless otherwise indicated, all images are from the author's collection.

INTRODUCTION

THE IRON CROSS was instituted in 1813, and is what is known as a 'temporary' award – one that is only presented when the nation is in a state of war. To be able to bestow this prestigious award, a formal renewal order was required. For this reason, different dates appear on the lower obverse arm of the Iron Cross, relating to the year of re-institution: the year 1813 on the reverse lower arm relates to the original institution date of the Order.

During the period from its institution to the end of World War I, a large 'gap' existed in the Iron Cross series of awards. There was no official interim decoration between the First Class, which could be awarded to soldiers of all ranks, and the Grand Cross, which was awarded only to senior commanders for winning a major battle or campaign. The gap was partly filled by awards given from Germany's constituent states: among the best known of these is the Pour le Merité or 'Blue Max' of Prussia. However, with the abdication of the Kaiser at the end of World War I, the awards granted by the various Royal households fell into abeyance.

A very rare example of the first type of Knight's Cross to be produced, immediately recognisable by the eyelet for the suspension loops. In other Knight's Cross examples this forms a complete circle, but in these early pieces it is only a half-circle. (Detlev Niemann)

In the autumn of 1939, when the Iron Cross was once again about to be re-instituted, it was clear that something would be required to fill this huge gap between the grades. Rather than using an unrelated award to bridge this gap, as had previously been the case, a new grade in the Iron Cross series was introduced, the Knight's Cross or *Ritterkreuz*. This was not an entirely new concept, as many of the decorations of the individual German states incorporated a Knight's Cross grade.

The Knight's Cross

The Knight's Cross of the Iron Cross (*Ritterkreuz des Eisernen Kreuzes*) was awarded for a very wide range of reasons. To illustrate by comparison, the range of gallantry and service awards to which a British soldier might aspire was quite large – the Victoria Cross, Military Cross, Distinguished Service Cross, Distinguished Service Order, Distinguished Flying Cross and Military Medal, to name but a few. The Knight's Cross, in contrast, rolled such wide-ranging awards into one, and with one particularly important distinction – it was bestowed across all ranks and grades, unlike many British medals, which had different and more attractive decorations for officers compared to those for the lower ranks. The Knight's Cross might be awarded to a senior commander for skilled leadership of his troops in battle, or to a humble private soldier for a single act of extreme gallantry. It could be awarded to an ace pilot for shooting down a high number of enemy aircraft, to a tank ace for destroying enemy armour, or to a submarine ace for sinking a high tonnage of enemy shipping. Between 1939 and 1945, some 7,282 awards of the Knight's Cross were made (the exact number is unknown, as records for the last hectic months of the war are incomplete). Although this might seem high, compared to the 182 awards of the Victoria Cross, the fact that the Knight's Cross was a wide-ranging award should be borne in mind. In addition, when considering the millions of soldiers who served in the course of the war, the Knight's Cross was clearly an extremely rare decoration.

The Knight's Cross holders were held in high regard, and the efficient German propaganda machine ensured a large amount of publicity was given to awardees. Young Germans could buy studio portrait photos of the latest winner to add to their collection. The winner might also be expected to make patriotic speeches to factory workers employed in the war effort, expressing thanks for the hard work of those on the home front, or alternatively might be asked to undertake a lecture tour.

Interestingly, the official term for one so decorated was *Ritterkreuzträger* or 'Knight's Cross Bearer', which almost suggests that the award was a burden. Many indeed saw this as the case, the burden being one of great responsibility to set an example to others. Suggestions had been made that the correct title for one decorated with this high award should be *Ritter des Eisernen Kreuz* or 'Knight of the Iron Cross'. Hitler refused to countenance this, believing that such a designation owed too much to titles granted by the Prussian aristocracy he despised so much.

A description of the Knight's Cross

The Knight's Cross was very similar in appearance to the Iron Cross Second Class. It was a *pattée* cross (one with flared, roughly triangular limbs) worn at the neck (*Am Halse*). It had a black, painted iron core: on its obverse was a central swastika with the year 1939 displayed in the lower arm. The black core was held within a two-part silver frame: the frame had a ribbed inner portion (with a matt silver finish) and a flat outer flange (with a highly burnished finish). The frame was usually struck from real silver, though plated examples do exist. On the top edge of the cross was a circular 'eye', struck as part of the frame rather than separately attached; a silver wire suspension loop was passed through this to accept the neck ribbon from which it was suspended. The original ribbon was 50mm wide with a wide red central stripe (exact dimensions vary) flanked in white and with a black edge stripe – red, white and black being the national colours during this period. At some early point during the war, 45mm-wide ribbon became the norm and surviving original examples of the Knight's Cross with 50mm ribbon are now rare.

When presented, the Knight's Cross came in a small case 123mm long, 80mm wide and 25mm deep, covered in black, leather-effect paper. The lid interior was lined in padded white satin and the base, recessed to the shape of the Cross and with a section for the neck ribbon, was covered in fine black velvet. The cased Cross was supplied by the manufacturer in a protective outer carton made of card, but these were usually discarded just before the award ceremony. Generally only those sent directly to the next of kin of posthumous awardees would retain the carton. The manufacture of the Knight's Cross was subject to very strict control, and consequently original examples are always of the highest quality.

Until mid-1941 Knight's Cross holders were able to purchase additional examples of the award through retail outlets such as uniform outfitters. It was then decided that any additional examples of such high decorations should only be available for purchase through official channels. Knight's Crosses lost or damaged in the course of duty would be replaced free of charge. It should also be noted that a number of recipients chose to keep the original award piece at home, and instead wore a converted example of the Iron Cross Second Class, which was cheap and easily obtained. Some wartime photos also show a pinback Iron Cross First Class attached at the neck. The vast majority of Knight's Cross recipients, however, proudly wore the original award pieces on all occasions and never had a substitute.

The award process and documents

A recommendation (*Vorschlag*) for the award of the Knight's Cross had to pass through many levels of scrutiny, for instance, the Divisional commander, the Korps commander, the Army Group, and so on, all the way to the Armed Forces High Command (*Oberkommando der Wehrmacht*). At each stage, the reviewing officer would add his comments supporting the *Vorschlag*, usually with ever more brief comments as it progressed up the chain of command. Ultimately, the recommendation would reach Hitler who would normally add a single comment: 'Approved!' (*Befurwortet!*) Many original examples of such recommendation papers, complete with the added comments of various senior commanders, still exist in the German Federal Archives and provide a fascinating insight into the award process.

As a first step, the recipient would be sent a brief telegram informing him of the award of the Knight's Cross, with a few words of congratulation. Sometime thereafter a preliminary certificate of possession (*Vorläufiges Besitzzeugnis*) would be sent. This award document came in a standardised, pre-printed format, on A5, buff-coloured stiff paper, with blank spaces left for the recipient's details to be filled in by typewriter. An example of the initial form can be found in Colour Plate A. The wording was as follows: 'The Fuhrer and Commander-in-Chief of the Armed Forces has awarded the Knight's Cross of the Iron Cross to [recipients name]'. Then followed

The standard wartime production Knight's Cross: this example was manufactured by C E Junker of Berlin and is shown in its original presentation case complete with the neck ribbon. The outer frame is burnished whilst the inner frame has a frosted matt finish. The iron centre is painted matt black, providing a very attractive contrast.

details of the date of the award, and the signature and ink stamp of the awarding authority. Award documents were printed in both Gothic (*Fraktur*) and Latin (*Latein*) script. Later award documents, in keeping with changes made to most military award documents simultaneously, saw the wording altered to simply: 'The Fuhrer has awarded...' with reference to Hitler's status as supreme commander of the Armed Forces dropped.

In the early part of the war, the preliminary certificate of possession was followed by a most elaborate formal award document, the *Ritterkreuzurkunde*. This was executed on a large sheet of parchment vellum, folded in half so as to effectively produce four sides, with the lettering on the 'third' side. The resultant 'pages' were approximately 43cm x 36cm. Also on the third page was a hand-drawn large eagle and swastika in rich brown ink. This was followed by the text: 'In the name of the German people...' followed by the recipient's name in gold lettering, with a representation of the Iron Cross and below that the name of the issuing authority and date. At the

foot of the page was the signature of Adolf Hitler. These signatures were often facsimiles, but on occasion are pen signatures executed by Hitler himself. These *Urkunden* were sent directly to the soldier's home address, not to his unit. A note of the award was also entered in the

OPPOSITE ABOVE **Occasionally, the Iron Cross Second Class was field-converted into the Knight's Cross by modifying the ribbon suspension, as shown here. This process provided a cheap and readily available ersatz Knight's Cross, for use until the formal award piece became available or to avoid damage to the proper item.**

OPPOSITE BELOW **The formal award document for the Knight's Cross of the Iron Cross (right), hand-executed on parchment vellum and contained within a hand-tooled leather folder (left). Original examples of these documents are now extremely rare. (Detlev Niemann)**

In most cases, the award of the Knight's Cross was carried out in the field, as shown here with a member of a Heer Sturm- geschütze and his commanding general.

soldier's ID book (*Soldbuch*), his military pass (*Wehrpass*) and personnel records. Examples of the document can be found in Colour Plate A and on page 6.

The document was contained in a large folder, covered in hand-tooled red Moroccan leather with a large embossed gold-leaf eagle on the front. The documents were produced by a team of the Reich's finest artisans and are works of great artistry. Unfortunately demand far outstripped the team's ability to supply these, and although many of those who earned the Knight's Cross in the first half of the war received one, later recipients were given only the preliminary certificate.

Oak-Leaves, Swords and Diamonds distinctions

As the war progressed, a range of further distinctions was created for bestowal on existing Knight's Cross winners, namely Oak-Leaves (*Eichenlaub*); Oak-Leaves with Swords (*Eichenlaub und Schwertern*); and Oak-Leaves with Swords and Diamonds (*Eichenlaub, Schwerter und Brillanten*), the latter being the most prestigious. Winners of the Oak-Leaves distinction in the period 1939–40 are covered in this volume. Future Elite-series titles will cover the background to and winners of the Knight's Cross with Oak-Leaves and Swords, and the introduction and 27 recipients of the Oak-Leaves with Swords and Diamonds award.

The Oak-Leaves distinction

The Oak-Leaves distinction was introduced in June 1940 to further distinguish those who had already won the Knight's Cross and who continued to show merit in combat bravery or military success. The silver clasp featured a motif of three leaves and was worn above the Cross, with the recipient removing the Cross's suspension ring and replacing it with the leaves. The leaves generally featured the manufacturer's mark on the rear. As per the Knight's Cross itself, the leaves were pre-sented in a leather box and with an award certificate. Eduard Dietl was the first recipient, in June 1941, following his exploits in Norway at Narvik. Approximately 880 Oak-Leaves distinctions were awarded during the war. A full discussion of the Oak-Leaves clasps will appear in the second volume of this sequence.

Distribution of the awards

By 1941, it had been decided that a significant gap existed between the Iron Cross First Class and the Knight's Cross. An award was required for deeds insufficient to justify the award of a Knight's Cross, but far more significant than those suited to the Iron Cross First Class. As a result, a further award known as the German Cross was instituted. This was not a part of the Iron Cross series, and there was no requirement for a soldier to possess the German Cross *before* earning the Knight's Cross. In fact although many soldiers did indeed earn their awards in the sequence Iron Cross First Class–German Cross–Knight's Cross, many others earned the Knight's Cross prior to the German Cross. For the remainder of the war, the German Cross and Knight's Cross, together with the small number

It was standard practice for a deceased soldier's awards to be displayed during his funeral service. Here the Knight's Cross and other awards of a Luftwaffe fighter pilot are carried by one of his comrades. (Terry Carter)

of Oak-Leaves and Oak-Leaves with Swords clasps, remained Germany's principal military decorations for gallantry and distinguished service.

Table 1 provides a comparison between major British gallantry awards in World War II and the combined figures for the Knight's Cross and German Cross.

Regulations for the award of the Iron Cross clearly stated that it was necessary for the previous grade to be held before the next grade could be earned. This rule, however, was simple to circumvent on the rare occasion that a soldier performed a single outstanding act of gallantry before even earning the lowly Iron Cross Second Class. On such occasions, the full set of Second Class, First Class and Knight's Cross were effectively awarded all at once, or with a day or so between them

for the sake of appearance. Such occasions, however, were very much the exception.

Table 2 provides a chronological breakdown of the Knight's Cross award process. These figures are not absolute, for a number of reasons. There was often a time gap between the approval of the award and its bestowal, so an award approved towards the end of one year might not actually be received until the following year. In addition, the situation in the late stages of the war became so chaotic that many soldiers had their awards approved but never received them. In some cases, individual soldiers did not find out that they had joined the ranks of the

In the case of U-boat captains, a long wait could ensue between the notification of the award of the Knight's Cross and the completion of a long war cruise, when the bestowal might take place. Here a successful U-boat commander is met at the dockside by his commanding admiral and presented with his award.

Table 1: Comparison between German and British awards			
German awards		*British awards*	
Oak-Leaves with Swords and Diamonds	27	Victoria Cross	182
Oak-Leaves with Swords	159	Military Cross	c.10,000
Oak-Leaves	882	Distinguished Flying Cross	c.20,000
Knight's Cross	6,214	Distinguished Service Cross	c.4,500
German Cross	c.40,000	Military Medal	c.15,000
		Distinguished Flying Medal	c.6,000
		Distinguished Service Medal	c.7,100
		Distinguished Conduct Medal	c.1,900
Total: c.47,282		**Total: c.64,682**	

Table 2: Chronology of award	
Year	*No. of awards*
1939	21
1940	440
1941	876
1942	952
1943	1,398
1944	2,448
1945	1,147
	Total: 7,282

Table 3: Branch award distribution	
Wehrmacht branch	No. of awards
Army	4,524
Luftwaffe	1,716
Waffen-SS	438
Kriegsmarine	318
Total: 6,996	

Table 4: Distribution by rank	
Rank	No. of awards
Schütze – Oberschütze	254
Unteroffizier – Stabsfeldwebel	1,422
Leutnant – Oberleutnant	1,908
Hauptmann	1,505
Major – Oberst	1,672
Generalmajor – Generalfeldmarschall	521
Total: 7,282	

Ritterkreuzträger until many years after the end of the war, as was the case with one awardee from the Grossdeutschland Division, who only discovered this on being invited to a post-war *Ritterkreuzträger* reunion. Nevertheless, the figures do reflect the general trend. Initially, awards were issued sparingly, but following the invasion of the Soviet Union, and with German troops involved in combat on many different fronts, the incidence of suitable situations increased dramatically. Following the Allied invasion of Normandy in 1944, the number of awards rose again, and in the final few months of the war peaked at over 280 per month.

Table 3 shows the distribution of award winners between the Wehrmacht's branches of service (this excludes the small number of awards to 'foreigners'). Given that the entire Wehrmacht fielded approximately 15 million soldiers during the course of World War II, the total of c.7,300 Knight's Cross winners creates an award ratio of 1:2,055. For the two smallest branches, the Waffen-SS and the Navy, the ratios were 1:2,280 and 1:2,830 respectively, so it can be seen that distribution of the award across the services was relatively even. Table 4 shows how distribution of the Knight's Cross between the ranks was also fairly balanced, with the bulk of the awards bestowed on ranks from Corporal (Unteroffizier) to Colonel (Oberst).

KNIGHT'S CROSS AND OAK-LEAVES RECIPIENTS

The award recipients in this section are representative of the most prominent type of awardee in the opening years of the war. They comprise high-ranking commanders decorated for their leadership during the highly successful opening phases; the fighter pilot and submarine aces who ran up enormous scores of enemy aircraft and ships destroyed; and the individual soldiers who displayed supreme bravery in combat. As the war progressed, the number of awards to senior officers for successful prosecution of a campaign dwindled, whilst those for acts of gallantry increased. Due to the restriction of space, the text (at least for senior commanders) concentrates on the point of award of the Knight's Cross. Many went on to receive further military honours, and the fortunes of some of those featured here will also appear in the subsequent volumes of this sequence of books.

Generalfeldmarschall Hermann Göring

Born in Marienbad on 1 December 1893, Hermann Wilhelm Göring served in the Imperial German Army with some distinction during World War I. He initially served in the infantry but transferred to the flying branch with the rank of Leutnant in 1914. He saw considerable

action on the Western Front, first as an observer and then as a fighter pilot, earning himself the coveted 'Pour le Merité' (popularly known as the 'Blue Max') in 1917. Göring served as commander of the famous Jagdstaffel Richthofen (Baron Manfred von Richthofen's 'Flying Circus') after the Red Baron's death. Though he became something of a figure of fun in later life there is no doubt that during his military service in World War I, he was a skilled, successful and gallant soldier.

Like many former professional soldiers during the inter-war period, Göring drifted into the Freikorps movement and was drawn to the NSDAP (National Socialist German Workers Party), which he joined in 1922. Hitler was delighted to have a highly decorated war hero in his entourage and Göring rose swiftly through the Nazi ranks, being appointed as commander of the SA Stormtroopers within months of being accepted into the Party. He married Karin von Kantzow, a woman

Hermann Göring as
Reichsmarschall and
Commander-in-Chief of the
Luftwaffe. The large upper cross
around his neck is the Grand
Cross of the Iron Cross. Below
that is his Blue Max and under
this is the Knight's Cross of the
Iron Cross awarded for his
command of the Luftwaffe
during the Polish campaign.
(Josef Charita)

to whom he was genuinely devoted, in 1923. Following the abortive Munich Putsch in November 1923, in which Göring was wounded, he fled the country. During the treatment of his wounds, however, he developed an addiction to morphine and this dependency on drugs was to play no small part in his deterioration from a fit and active former soldier to an obese figure of fun, albeit one for whom most Germans retained a modicum of affection for much of the war. Following an amnesty for those involved in the Putsch, Göring returned to Germany in 1926 and within two years had been elected to serve as a member of the Reichstag, the German government. Göring's wife Karin died in 1931. He remarried in April 1935, to actress Emmy Sonneman, though his vast estate was named Karinhall after his first wife.

After the Nazi accession to power, Göring's status and power grew. He became overall commander of the German Air Sports League (*Deutsche Luftsports Verband* or DLV), a 'cover' organisation surreptitiously training future German airforce pilots. When the new German air force, the Luftwaffe, was officially unveiled in 1935, Göring was at its head. In line with his flamboyant personality, he revelled in having special 'one-off' uniforms and insignia designed for his personal use, and threw lavish parties on his estate, where he often wore a Roman toga and showed his pet lions to visitors. He was also a keen hunter, and held the title of Master of the Hunt (Reichsjägermeister). Despite Göring's indiscreet and lavish lifestyle, Hitler was content to continue his patronage of the former fighter ace, whose popularity with the people provided him with an 'acceptable face' of Nazism. Behind the jovial mask, however, he was utterly ruthless. Indeed, it was Göring, as head of the Prussian State Police, who founded the Gestapo.

During the second half of the 1930s, Göring's Luftwaffe had been built into an immensely powerful force with a vast fleet of fighters, medium bombers and dive-bombers. German aircraft were in general at least the equal if not superior to those available to any of her potential future enemies. As well as holding the rank of Commander-in-Chief of the Airforce (Oberbefehlshaber der Luftwaffe), Göring held the post of Minister of Aviation (Reichsminister der Luftfahrt).

When civil war broke out in Spain in 1936, Germany lost no time in offering aid to Franco's Nationalists and Göring was happy to despatch a significant force of fighter and bomber aircraft, effectively allowing his Luftwaffe a 'full dress rehearsal' for any coming war in Europe. Many of the great German fighter aces actually earned their status well before World War II, having shot down five or more Republican aircraft in Spain.

In 1938, Göring was promoted from General to the rank of Generalfeldmarschall. When World War II broke out in September 1939, the Luftwaffe played a major part in the subjugation of Poland. Bombers laid waste to Warsaw and other major Polish towns; German fighters quickly eliminated any Polish resistance with many Polish aircraft being destroyed on the ground before they could be brought into action. It was, however, the Junkers 87 'Stuka' dive-bomber that came to symbolise German air-power during the years of blitzkrieg. In almost vertical dives, with the air rushing through the sirens mounted on their undercarriage producing an unearthly howling, the Stuka was to prove a highly effective psychological as well as military weapon. With the Polish campaign brought to a successful conclusion in just 36 days, Hitler recognised the part played in this success by Göring's Luftwaffe: on 30 September 1939, Göring became one of the first recipients of the new Knight's Cross of the Iron Cross for his command role. In the 1940 campaigns, which brought about the fall of France and the Low Countries and the defeat of the British Expeditionary Force, the Luftwaffe once more played a crucial role. Göring was singularly honoured with promotion to the rank of Reichsmarschall, and on 19 July 1940 was awarded the Grand Cross of the Iron Cross – the only one to be awarded in World War II.

General der Flieger Albert Kesselring

Albert Kesselring was born in Marktsheft on 20 November 1885. He joined the army as an officer cadet at the age of 23 and served in the 2nd Bavarian Foot Artillery Regiment. During the course of World War I, Kesselring served as a balloon observer – an extremely dangerous role. Whilst on the Western Front he met and developed a strong and lasting friendship with the then fighter pilot Hermann Göring. Transferring to the Eastern Front in 1918 he served as a divisional staff officer. He remained in military service after the end of World War I and became chief of staff to the defence minister. By 1932 he had achieved the rank of Generalmajor. One year later he transferred to the air force as a civilian director of administration, where he served under General Erhard Milch. His friendship with the commander-in-chief stood him in good stead, however, and in 1937 he was personally appointed by Göring as Chief of Staff of the Luftwaffe.

With the attack on Poland in September 1939, Kesselring was appointed commander of Luftflotte 1. In recognition of the part played by his forces in the success of the campaign, he was decorated with the Knight's Cross on 30 September that year. In 1940, Kesselring transferred to command Luftflotte 2 during the *Westfeldzug* (the Western campaign) and throughout the Battle of Britain. He was promoted to the rank of Generalfeldmarschall in July 1940.

With the invasion of the Soviet Union in 1941, Kesselring took his Air Fleet eastwards but in

Generalfeldmarschall Albert Kesselring – known as 'Smiling Albert', for obvious reasons. This photograph shows him in tropical service dress during his tenure as Commander-in-Chief of German forces in the Mediterranean. The award around his neck is actually the Oak-Leaves Swords and Diamonds Clasp awarded to him in 1943. (Josef Charita)

December of that year was appointed commander of all German air and
land forces in the Mediterranean. He oversaw the attack on Malta and
supported Rommel's forces in North Africa. Kesselring also commanded
German forces in Italy during the retreat there, his troops coming very
close to thwarting the Allied successes at Salerno and Anzio. He was
commander-in-chief of German forces in Italy as well as of Army Group
C (Heeresgruppe C). He was seriously injured in a road accident in
October 1944 but post-recovery returned to Italy in 1945, and was
appointed by Hitler as Supreme Commander South (Oberbefehlshaber
Süd).

At war's end, he was charged with war crimes in respect of reprisal
killings carried out by SS troops on Hitler's orders whilst he was
commander in Italy. He was sentenced to death but this was commuted to
life imprisonment and he was released soon afterwards due to his failing
health: he died on 16 July 1960. Kesselring was one of Germany's most
decorated soldiers. After the award of the Knight's Cross he went on to
earn the Oak-Leaves, Oak-Leaves with Swords and the rare Oak-Leaves
with Swords and Diamonds.

Grossadmiral Erich Raeder

Erich Raeder was born on 24 April 1876 in Wandsbek in the province of Schleswig-Holstein. In 1894, aged 18, he joined the navy and rose rapidly through the ranks to become Chief of Staff to Admiral Hipper. During World War I he saw considerable combat action, and was present at the Battle of Doggerbank in 1915 and at Jutland in 1916. By the end of the war he had his own command as captain of the cruiser *Cöln*.

With the German armed forces reduced to a mere 100,000 men by the terms of the Treaty of Versailles, Raeder was fortunate to find himself retained by the newly formed Reichsmarine where he served on with the rank of Kapitän zur See. His rapid progress continued, despite the restrictions on career development options in the tiny armed forces of the Weimar Republic, and he was promoted Konteradmiral in charge of training in 1922. In 1924 he was appointed commander-in-chief of light naval units (Oberbefehlshaber leichte Seestreitkräfte) and in the following year was given command of German naval units in the Baltic. In 1928 he was promoted to full Admiral and commander-in-chief of the German Navy.

Although the Kriegsmarine did not play a significant role in the Polish campaign (which it mostly spent blockading the exits from the Baltic in an attempt to ensure Polish warships did not escape into the Atlantic), it did fire the opening shots of the war when the elderly battleship *Schleswig-Holstein* bombarded the Polish fortress at Westerplatte in Danzig. Marine infantry then stormed and captured the fortress. As commander-in-chief of the Navy, and in recognition of the (comparatively minor) part played by the Kriegsmarine in the German military successes so far, Grossadmiral Raeder was decorated with the Knight's Cross on 30 September 1939.

Raeder's tenure as commander-in-chief lasted until 1943 when he had a major disagreement with the Führer. Hitler threatened to decommission all major units of the surface fleet and have their guns unshipped for use on land. Rader resigned in protest, to be replaced by the Commander-in-Chief Submarines, Karl Dönitz. Raeder retained the post of

This early photograph shows Raeder escorting Hitler during a formal visit by the Führer to units of the Reichsmarine. Note that Raeder's peaked cap does not yet bear the National Socialist eagle and swastika insignia, dating this picture to pre-1935. Though far from enamoured with the Nazis, Raeder saw it as his duty as a soldier to serve his government loyally.

Admiralinspekteur der Kriegsmarine but was effectively in retirement for the remainder of the war.

Generalfeldmarschall Gerd von Rundstedt

Gerd von Rundstedt was born on 12 December 1875 in Aschersleben, and was the son of a career Army officer. He served in the Imperial German Army, reaching the rank of major by the end of World War I. He remained in military service after the war, and in 1932 was given command of 3.Infanterie-Division. Rundstedt was very much anti-Hitler, and tried to prevent Nazi-sympathising officers from being awarded positions of power. Frustrated at their growing influence within the German military, he resigned his commission in October 1938.

On the outbreak of war in September 1939, at the age of 64, von Rundstedt found himself recalled for service with the rank of Generaloberst: he was given command of Army Group North (Heeresgruppe Nord) during the attack on Poland. Von Rundstedt was another of the top-level commanders and senior officers decorated for his part in the Polish campaign, receiving the Knight's Cross on 30 September 1939. Subsequently, he was appointed Supreme Commander of German Forces in the East, but did not take well to the activities of the security and SS troops in the occupied areas, and was transferred to the West at his own request.

Von Rundstedt, being a soldier of the 'old school', was far from convinced by the blitzkrieg concept of fast mobile warfare espoused by men like Guderian. He was in fact instrumental in persuading Hitler to halt the rapid advance of the Panzer Divisions so that the infantry following could catch up with them. Had von Rundstedt not insisted on

Generaloberst Gerd von Rundstedt shown just after the award of the Knight's Cross for his command of Army Group South during the campaign in Poland. It is interesting to note that this 'old-school' soldier wears the patches of his honorary status as colonel in chief of Infanterie-Regiment 18, as opposed to the collar patches of a Wehrmacht general. (Josef Charita)

a conventional assault on the British enclave at Dunkirk, with the Panzers supported by infantry, the great escape of the BEF might never have taken place. Despite this lost opportunity, von Rundstedt was promoted to Generalfeldmarschall on 19 July 1940 in the aftermath of the overall success of the Western campaign.

Von Rundstedt was given command of Army Group South during the attack on the Soviet Union, and was involved in the capture of the city of Kiev and along with it over 650,000 enemy prisoners. During the advance, he suffered a heart attack but refused to be evacuated and continued his march into Russia. He reached Rostov in late-November but here the enemy counter-attacked and his troops were forced back. He infuriated Hitler by demanding permission to retreat and was sacked.

Von Rundstedt was recalled once again in March 1942 and given command of troops defending the Atlantic Wall. He was still in this post when the Allies landed in Normandy in June 1944, and once again infuriated Hitler by insisting that a peace settlement be negotiated. Hitler sacked him once again. He was, however, further decorated with the award

of Oak-Leaves to his Knight's Cross in July 1944, and Swords in February 1945. Despite his disagreements with Hitler, his qualities as a senior commander were clearly respected. Von Rundstedt was captured in May 1945 and suffered a second heart attack. He was released from prison in July 1948 and lived in Hannover until his death in 1953.

General der Panzertruppe Heinz Guderian

Guderian was born in Culm, West Prussia, on 17 June 1888. In 1908, at the age of 20, he completed training at the Kriegsschule in Metz, and was commissioned into a Hannoverian Light Infantry Battalion. Having served first as a signals officer and then as a staff officer during World War I, during which time he won both the second and first classes of the Iron Cross, he found himself retained by the post-war Reichswehr. Guderian's speciality was military transport and he quickly developed a strong interest and considerable expertise in tanks.

Although his enthusiasm for armour was opposed by the more traditionalist officers in the high command of the German Army, who saw tanks purely as support weapons for the infantry, Guderian had a powerful supporter in Hitler. After seeing an exercise involving tanks, armoured cars and motorcycles laid on by Guderian to demonstrate a more flexible use of armour, the Fürher exclaimed: 'That is what I need!'

In 1938, Guderian was appointed Chef der Schnelle Truppen, and made responsible for recruitment and training of armoured and motorised units. By the outbreak of war he had been promoted to the rank of General der Panzertruppen. During the Polish campaign his Panzers (XIX Korps) were used exactly as he had envisaged – fast, spearhead units supported by aircraft and motorised infantry all on a narrow front – and worked almost to perfection. His Panzertruppe smashed their way through Polish resistance all the way to Brest-Litovsk, and as a result Guderian was decorated with the Knight's Cross on 27 October 1939.

The attack on France and the Low Countries in 1940 gave Guderian another opportunity to prove the validity of the blitzkrieg concept. His Panzers were constantly at the forefront of the advance, with Guderian right up there with them – at the crossing of the Meuse, at Sedan, and on reaching the Channel coast – and he played a significant part overall in the success of both campaigns. Guderian still had his detractors in the high command of the Army and was ordered to halt his tanks on several occasions to allow following infantry units to catch up, most notably at Dunkirk, where the delay allowed a large part of the BEF to escape.

Guderian was a modern, forward-thinking officer, and a firm believer in the blitzkrieg concept. He often clashed with traditionalist superiors, and did not suffer fools gladly. Guderian also had frequent arguments with Hitler, rarely pulling his punches when expressing opinions on important matters. (Josef Charita)

In 1941, Guderian's Panzergruppe II led the advance on Moscow, making excellent progress despite the loss of many tanks through mechanical breakdown: the rapid advance over huge tracts of land placed a great strain on them. The phenomenal successes of his armoured units during the initial phases of Operation BARBAROSSA brought the addition of Oak-Leaves to Guderian's Knight's Cross on 17 July 1941. He was enraged when Hitler diverted his tanks south into the Ukraine, knowing that the success of the drive on Moscow was being put at risk. This resulted in a bitter dispute with Hitler, with Guderian being accused of insubordination as a consequence. It was to be the first of several such conflicts. When the advance on Moscow faltered, as Guderian had predicted it would, he was sacked – one of Hitler's many scapegoats. Guderian was recalled and appointed Generalinspekteur der Panzertruppen in 1943. He did much to modernise and improve the tank arm but had regular arguments with Hitler, refusing to become one of Hitler's sycophantic entourage. He was sacked once again in March 1945.

Kapitänleutnant Günther Prien

The first of Germany's great U-boat aces was born in Osterfeld on 16 January 1908. His naval career began when he joined the Merchant Navy in 1923 at the age of just 15. Working his way up from a humble cabin boy, at the age of 23 he gained his master's ticket, enabling him to serve as a Fourth Officer on large passenger ships. His career, however, was cut short in 1932 when, like so many of his countrymen, he became unemployed following cut-backs to the merchant navy caused by Germany's dire economic straits.

He immediately enlisted into the Reichsmarine, though this required him to revert back to the rank of Ordinary Seaman. His experience and personal qualities ensured he soon regained lost ground and by 1935 he had gained a commission as Leutnant zur See and a transfer to the new U-boat arm of the Navy, now renamed the Kriegsmarine. After two years of intensive training on U-boats, Prien was promoted to Oberleutnant zur See. He obtained priceless active service experience on patrols during the Spanish Civil War as a Watch Officer on *U-26*. Prien was rapidly building a reputation as a fearless and aggressive officer, always scoring highly on training exercises. His dedication paid off when, in December 1938, Prien at last gained his own command, the Type VIIB boat *U-47*. In March 1939 he was promoted to Kapitänleutnant.

Following the outbreak of war, Prien immediately began to satisfy the high expectations of his superiors. On 5 September, he sank his first enemy ship during his first patrol, the British freighter *Bosnia*: Prien ensured that the crew were safely evacuated and handed over to a neutral ship before sinking the 2,400-ton vessel. Not one single life was lost. Two more freighters totalling just under 6,000 tons were sunk during this patrol. Prien was a committed Nazi supporter, but this did not prevent him from carrying out his duties in as chivalrous a manner as circumstances allowed.

Meanwhile, the Commanding Admiral Submarines, Konteradmiral Karl Dönitz, had been planning a strike at the very heart of the British Navy's home fleet, the anchorage at Scapa Flow in the Orkneys. A daring and audacious commander would be needed for such a task, and Prien was offered the opportunity. In a night-time attack on 13 October, Prien was able to navigate

As one of Germany's greatest war heroes, Günther Prien was immortalised in many paintings. This one, showing him in his U-boat leather jacket and white-topped commander's cap, was painted by the famous war artist Wilhelm Willrich, and formed part of an extensive series of period colour postcards for collectors. (Josef Charita)

his boat through the defended entrance to Scapa Flow where he torpedoed and sank the battleship *Royal Oak* before escaping unscathed. Although being somewhat elderly and not one of the Royal Navy's finest ships, the loss of the *Royal Oak*, to say nothing of the 833 crew lost too, torpedoed by an enemy submarine in what was considered a safe anchorage, was a devastating blow to British morale. Many refused to believe a submarine had been responsible and rumours of sabotage circulated for years afterwards. On his return to Germany, Prien was decorated with both the Iron Cross First Class and the Knight's Cross of the Iron Cross in recognition of his great achievement. In fact the entire crew of *U-47* were decorated with the Second Class Iron Cross (First Class for those who already held the Second Class) and were invited to a formal reception in Berlin hosted by Hitler. The crew of *U-47*, especially Prien, became heroes overnight.

Prien's next war cruise was also a success, setting off from Kiel on 16 November and sinking a further three enemy ships in a month-long voyage, returning to base just before the end of the year. After a spell in dry-dock for repairs and maintenance, *U-47* set out on its fourth war cruise, which in the event was rather uneventful with only one enemy ship sunk. The fifth patrol was also unsuccessful, *U-47* being dogged by recurring problems with torpedoes. The torpedo crisis was affecting all U-boat commanders who were forced to watch helplessly as time after time they detonated prematurely, or failed to detonate at all (caused by insufficient testing of the complex magnetic detonators on the torpedoes). Worst of all was the fact that a premature detonation would fail to damage the enemy ship but would immediately alert enemy escorts to the presence of the U-boat, and several were lost to counter-attacks by British escorts.

By the time Prien set out on his sixth patrol in June 1940, conventional impact pistols had been retro-fitted to the torpedoes and Prien once again achieved dramatic results. In a cruise lasting some 34 days, *U-47* sank eight

enemy ships, thus adding some 51,000 tons to his score. His seventh cruise was almost as successful, a further seven enemy ships being sunk, and a further 35,000 tons added to his tally. Prien's audacious manner was well illustrated during his eighth patrol: after a successful attack on a British convoy that netted him three more victims, he had only one torpedo remaining, and was assigned to act as a weather monitoring boat. During this period he detected a further British convoy and called in a number of other U-boats to make the attack. Despite being ordered to return to port, Prien did not wish to lose the opportunity to make good use of his remaining torpedo. He joined in the attack and sank a further enemy ship, before surfacing and seriously damaging another with his deck gun. On his ninth patrol, a short run lasting just ten days, he added a further four enemy vessels to his growing list of victims.

On 20 October 1940 Prien became only the fifth German to win the coveted Oak-Leaves clasp addition to the Knight's Cross. At this point *U-47* was taken into port for a long-overdue refit and Dönitz took the opportunity to offer Prien a transfer to a shore-based post in command of a training unit where his vast experience could be put to good use. Prien refused and insisted on staying with his boat. On 5 February 1941, during his tenth patrol, Prien encountered a British convoy and growing impatient with the wait for reinforcements to arrive (these were despatched when the convoy was detected), Prien attacked alone. Three ships were sunk and a further damaged. Prien then acted as a homing point for a squadron of Focke-Wulf 'Condor' maritime bombers, which sunk a further seven of the enemy's ships. On 29 February, when still at sea, Prien was promoted to the rank of Korvettenkapitän.

On 7 March, Prien began yet another convoy attack. He successfully torpedoed a large whaling ship, but then came under attack himself from British escorts. What happened next is not clear, but it is likely that *U-47* fell victim to a depth-charge attack by the British escorts *Wolverine* and *Verity*. Germany had lost the first of its great U-boat aces. The Nazi propaganda machine had elevated him to a national hero, with a book published of his exploits (almost certainly written 'on his behalf' by a member of the propaganda ministry) and even a film made based on some of his experiences. Prien himself was somewhat bemused by all this, and made it clear that in his own eyes, he was 'an officer, not a movie star'. In addition to the Knight's Cross with Oak-Leaves, he was decorated with the U-boat Badge with Diamonds and the diamond-studded Navy Honour Dagger. His final tally was 30 enemy ships sunk and six more damaged for a total of 165,000 tons, in addition to the sinking of the *Royal Oak*.

Kapitänleutnant Engelbert Endrass

Engelbert 'Bertl' Endrass was born in Bamberg on 2 March 1911. Another former officer in the Merchant Navy who transferred to the Kriegsmarine, Endrass joined the U-boat branch in 1937. He saw service on non-intervention patrolling during the Spanish Civil War and was decorated with the Spanish Cross in Bronze.

Endrass joined the crew of *U-47* as a Leutnant zur See and Watch Officer under the command of Günther Prien and was part of *U-47*'s crew that sunk the *Royal Oak* at Scapa Flow. Under the tutelage of the great ace, Endrass was allowed to develop and hone his own skills on three war cruises with *U-47*, to say nothing of earning the Iron Cross in both Second and First classes. Finally, in December 1939, he was sent on a U-boat commander training course and in May 1940, as an Oberleutnant zur See, was given command of his own boat, *U-46*.

A fine portrait study of Engelbert Endrass. Endrass learned his craft well under Prien. When his Knight's Cross was awarded he was referred to in several publicity announcements as 'ein schuler Priens' ('one of Prien's pupils'). The astonishing successes achieved by Endrass, however, suggest that, had he lived longer, he may well have surpassed his tutor. (Josef Charita)

On his first war cruise as a commander in his own right, Endrass sank five enemy ships totalling over 35,000 tons, one of which was an armed auxiliary cruiser, HMS *Carinthia*. His second war cruise coincidentally netted the same number of victims, with incredibly, yet another armed auxiliary cruiser, this time HMS *Dunvegan Castle*, and brought his total to over 60,000 tons sunk. On his return from his second war cruise, on 6 September 1940, he was decorated with the Knight's Cross of the Iron Cross. Endrass continued his successful command of *U-46*: his score reached 133,800 tons sunk, and on 10 June 1941 he was awarded the Oak-Leaves for his Knight's Cross – only the 14th soldier of the Armed Forces to be so decorated. Shortly afterwards he also received the U-boat Badge with Diamonds from Grossadmiral Raeder.

In July 1941, Endrass was promoted to Kapitänleutnant zur See and was given command of a new boat, *U-567*. However, with this transfer Endrass's luck ran out. On 21 December 1941, during its first war cruise, Endrass was directed to attack a newly located convoy. He managed to sink a 3,300 ton steamer, but was then attacked by British escort vessels HMS *Deptford* and HMS *Sapphire* north of the Azores. *U-567* was sunk with all hands. His tally of enemy shipping sunk stood

Endrass is shown here with his crew during the so-called 'Indienststellung', or formal commissioning ceremony, in which the U-boat (in this case *U-48*) was accepted into the Navy after extensive trials and crew training.

Endrass too was immortalised in art. This painting shows him on the bridge of his U-boat, binoculars in hand. The leather deck coat he wears was typical of the clothing much favoured by seagoing personnel, and especially by members of the U-boat flotillas. (Josef Charita)

at over 137,000 tons – an incredible achievement, considering this was amassed in a little over 18 months. At that point it was also one of the highest scores of enemy shipping sunk. Had he survived there seems little doubt that he would have gone on to become one of the greatest of all the U-boat aces.

Oberleutnant Alfred Schwarzmann

Born in Fürth on 23 March 1912, Alfred Schwarzmann began his military career with the infantry. He enlisted into the Reichswehr on 1 April 1929, signing up for a minimum service period of 12 years, and soon reached NCO rank. He was a keen sportsman, and represented Germany in gymnastics during the 1936 Berlin Olympics, winning three Olympic Gold Medals. His extremely high level of physical fitness and gymnastic ability led to him being posted as an instructor at the Army Sports School in Wünsdorf.

Schwarzmann transferred to the paratroops in January 1939, joining II.Bataillon, Fallschirmjäger-Regiment 1 at the paratroop training grounds at Stendal. He was the very epitome of the Fallschirmjäger: young, determined, brave and super-fit. After attending officer school Schwarzmann was commissioned as a Leutnant and in March 1940 was promoted to Oberleutnant and given command of a machine gun platoon in 8.Kompanie of the same regiment. On 10 May 1940, Schwarzmann and his platoon were dropped into Holland, the battalion assembling near the Moerdijk bridges: these were swiftly captured, with the Dutch guards being taken completely by surprise. The Dutch, however, were determined to recapture their position and launched counter-attacks. Schwarzmann and his men hung on tenaciously, Schwarzmann himself receiving a bullet wound to the lung. Eventually, German reinforcements arrived, relieving the wounded officer and his men and securing the bridge. On 25 May 1940, Schwarzmann received both the Second and First Class Iron Crosses, followed on 29 May by the Knight's Cross of the Iron Cross for his determined defence of the captured positions despite his own serious wounds.

Schwarzmann, like so many of his comrades from the *Westfeldzug,* saw action during the invasion of Crete and on the Eastern Front. He was promoted to Hauptmann in June 1942 and subsequently commanded the company of which his former platoon had been part. In the spring of 1943, he was posted to a staff position with the headquarters of 7.Flieger-Division, before moving on to 1.Fallschirm-Division. A year later he was hospitalised due to complications from his lung wound and spent some time out of active service. He was promoted to major in April 1945. Despite his wounds, Schwarzmann maintained his passion for athletics post-war and in 1952, once again represented his country at the Helsinki Olympic games winning, at the age of 40, a very creditable Silver Medal. He died in March 2000 at the age of 88.

The award of the Knight's Cross to Schwarzmann is not without controversy. It has been claimed that he did nothing of particular note during the action for which he was decorated, and that when he was seriously wounded and looked likely to die, the award of the Knight's Cross was made purely for propaganda reasons to create a Fallschirmjäger 'hero'. To compound matters, Schwarzmann is said to have been extremely boastful of his award, losing the respect of many of his comrades.

Alfred Schwarzmann, an Olympic athlete who served with considerable courage and distinction as a member of the elite Fallschirmjäger-Regiment 1. (Josef Charita)

Fregattenkapitän Otto Kretschmer

Otto Kretschmer was probably the greatest of the World War II U-boat aces. He was born in Heidau, Silesia, on 1 May 1912. As a young man, before commencing his maritime career, he spent some time in Great Britain where he developed a fluent command of the English language. Entering the Navy in 1930, he underwent the usual officer training of his day, which included service 'before the mast' in a sail training ship, a luxury unavailable to many who joined the navy during wartime, and a world cruise on the training ship *Emden*, a light cruiser. After gaining his commission in October 1934, Kretschmer spent two years on the light cruiser *Köln*, before volunteering to transfer to the fledgling U-boat service. Kretschmer's first command was *U-35*, and although this was only for a short period, it did allow him some operational experience on

This portrait of 'Silent Otto' Kretschmer shows him wearing the Oak-Leaves with Swords on his Knight's Cross. However, the award was not presented to him until after his capture: this photo is actually an earlier shot of him wearing the Oak-Leaves only, which has been skillfully retouched by the photographer's studio.

non-intervention patrols during the Spanish Civil War, before taking command of *U-23*. This was a tiny Type II coastal boat, given the derogatory nickname of 'Canoes' by the sailors due to their diminutive size.

Between the outbreak of war and 1 April 1940, Kretschmer completed eight cruises in *U-23*, accounting for over 100 days at sea. His first operational sorties were minelaying operations off the British coast, and it was not until 12 January 1940 that he attacked his first enemy ship, sinking the 10,000-ton tanker *Danmark*. In February of 1940, Kretschmer attacked and sunk the British destroyer HMS *Daring*. In April of the same year, Kretschmer took command of a fresh new submarine, the Type VII vessel *U-99*, and began a two-month period of intensive training before taking her out on her first war cruise in June 1940. During this he was attacked by one of the Arado floatplanes from the battlecruiser *Scharnhorst*, which mistook him for an enemy submarine. *U-99* suffered serious damage to her periscope, but survived the attack.

Kretschmer quickly began to make a name for himself as a skilled and daring commander. He was a pioneer of the principle that for a night attack it was safer and more effective to take the U-boat on the surface right into the midst of the convoy: the tiny silhouette of the U-boat sat low in the water, and in the darkness was very difficult for observers high up on the enemy ships to spot. Kretschmer was also a skilled marksman, whose motto was 'one torpedo, one ship'. Naturally, being right in amongst the enemy ships and firing at what amounted to point-blank range was bound to bring more success. It did, however, require ice-cool nerves and considerable skill. On one occasion, Kretschmer came under attack from enemy escort vessels and endured a 14-hour sustained attack in which over 120 depth charges were dropped.

Otto Kretschmer earned himself the nickname *schweigsame Otto*, or 'Silent Otto', for his quiet demeanour. Kretschmer also insisted that he, his officers and his men made every effort to keep their appearance as smart as possible. Indeed he pioneered the use of smart U-boat overalls, by simply commandeering captured supplies of lightweight denim British battledress that had fallen into German hands after the battle for France. (The Germans later made their own almost exact copies of this British uniform.) Incidentally, the typical image seen in wartime photos of U-boat commanders and their crews as scruffy, unshaven, almost piratical looking men wearing a mixture of military and civilian clothing, is actually fairly accurate. Water was too precious a commodity on a long war cruise to be wasted on shaving, and most U-boat commanders were more interested in their men operating at peak efficiency than they were in them looking smart and well dressed. The environment in an operational U-boat on a war cruise did not

Kretschmer as he would typically appear during an operational cruise on *U-99*. Unlike many U-boat captains who would forego shaving during a war cruise, and by the end of the mission look more like a bearded pirate of old, Kretschmer insisted on always looking as smart as circumstances would allow. Here he wears captured British battledress of lightweight denim, far more suitable for wear inside a submarine than the normal blue naval officer's uniform jacket.

encourage sailors to wear regulation 'blues'. However they may have looked, U-boat men were extremely well disciplined, each knowing that his own and his crewmates' lives depended on him obeying the captain's orders instantly and without hesitation.

On 4 August 1940 Kretschmer was decorated with the Knight's Cross for having sunk over 120,000 tons of enemy shipping: in one single patrol in November 1940, he destroyed two British armed auxiliary cruisers, HMS *Patroclus* and HMS *Laurentic*, these alone totalling over 30,000 tons. On 4 November 1940, Kretschmer was awarded the Oak-Leaves for his Knight's Cross for his outstanding successes. Before long, he was the unquestioned 'king' of enemy tonnage sunk, and in fact his tally was never surpassed. (Only a tiny number of the great submarine aces of the Kaiser's Navy in World War I exceeded Kretschmer's score – and they were operating against virtually no effective anti-submarine measures.)

Kretschmer was promoted to Korvettenkapitän effective 1 March 1941. On 17 March 1941 during his tenth war patrol, Kretschmer was forced to surface after his boat was badly damaged by depth charges dropped by HMS *Walker*. Immediate arrangements were put into effect to ensure the boat sank immediately after the crew abandoned ship, to prevent its capture by the enemy. Fortunately in the circumstances, only three of the 43-man crew were lost. Kretschmer and the remainder were picked up and taken into captivity. At the time of his capture Kretschmer had sunk 39 enemy ships (and damaged several others) representing a total of around 266,000 tons. He ultimately found his way to a POW camp in Canada, where he became the senior German officer. Swords were added to his Oak-Leaves on 26 December 1941 whilst he was in captivity, news of the award being passed on to Kretschmer by the Canadian camp commandant.

The C-in-C U-boats, Admiral Karl Dönitz, was keen to see Kretschmer at liberty once more and devised a plan to have a U-boat collect him and other escaped prisoners if they could break out of the camp itself. Canadian money, forged documents, maps, train schedules, and charts of Canada's east coast were smuggled in to the camp. The prisoners dug a complex system of tunnels under the camp using shovels made from tin cans, and storing soil in the cuffs of their trouser turn-ups, to be raked back into the ground outside. Soil was also stored in the ceilings of the accommodation huts. Unfortunately for Kretschmer, one of his fellow prisoners, a keen gardener, was working in the camp's flower-beds when his shovel broke through the soil, and he fell through into the tunnel. Kretschmer at the time was sitting in the tunnel waiting for the right moment to make his break. The U-boat ace spent the next 28 days in solitary confinement and the remaining years of the war in the same camp. On 1 September 1944, he was promoted to the rank of Fregattenkapitän: he remained in captivity until after the war.

A mid-war E-boat. Knicknamed the 'Greyhounds of the Sea', these boats were extremely fast and packed a much heavier punch than Allied equivalents (such as the Motor Torpedo Boat, or MTB) they often encountered in operations in the English Channel. 'E-boat' (from 'enemy boat') was the Allied term for this vessel, whereas the Germans called it the S-Boote (from Schnellboot, or 'fast boat').

In December 1947 Kretschmer was released and returned to Germany. In 1955 he joined the post-war West German Bundesmarine and in 1957 became commander of the 1st Escort Squadron. In November 1958 he became commander of all Amphibian Forces. From 1962 he served in a number of staff positions before becoming Chief of Staff of the NATO Command in May 1965, a post he held until 1969. When he finally retired in 1970 he had attained the rank of Flotillenadmiral and was one of Germany's most respected sailors. In the summer of 1998 during a vacation in Bavaria, Otto Kretschmer died in hospital after being involved in an accident.

Korvettenkapitän Rudolf Petersen

Petersen was born on 15 June 1905 in Atzerballig. He joined the Reichsmarine at the age of 20 in 1925 and progressed rapidly. By 1938 he held the post of Chief of 2.Schnellbootsflotille. This flotilla was initially equipped with a version of the E-boat equipped with extremely unreliable MAN diesel engines. Petersen and his flotilla were based in Heligoland at this time. The poor-quality boats were passed over to the training flotilla and new boats allocated to 2.Schnellbootsflotille but extremely bad weather conditions and the re-equipping with the new boats kept the flotilla out of action for the remainder of 1939.

By the spring of 1940, 2.Schnellbootsflotille was operating out of Borkum, attacking Allied shipping, and often coming under fire from RAF fighter bombers on their way to and from operations. Despite numerous claims, no British ships were sunk at this time though the E-boats' 'nuisance' effect was considerable. On 29 May, however, acting alongside vesels from 1.Schnellbootsflotille, Petersen's boats were responsible for sinking the British destroyer HMS *Wakeful*. On the following day, the French destroyers *Siroco* and *Cyclone* also fell victim to the E-boats.

Following the successful conclusion of the campaign in the West, however, the Kriegsmarine was presented with a number of operational bases on the Channel coast, and began regular operations against British shipping. Throughout June, Petersen's boats were in action against British convoys, notably sinking the 3,000-ton steamer *Roseburn*. Throughout July and August, 2 S-Bootsflotille was heavily involved in minelaying operations, carrying out 11 separate sorties and laying over 130 mines. On 8 August 1940, Kapitän zur See Petersen was decorated with the Knight's Cross of the Iron Cross in recognition of the performance of the flotilla under his command. Although at this time the flotilla had not yet sunk a huge tonnage of enemy shipping, the E-boats were proving to be a considerable thorn in the side of the British and greatly stretched British resources by requiring protection for

Rudolf Petersen, the Commander of E-boats, was a highly skilled officer, both as commander of his own boat, and later at flotilla and higher levels. Petersen was also involved in redesigning the war badge issued to E-boat crews when a new version was produced in 1943. (Josef Charita)

shipping. As the war progressed, the E-boats would be second only to the U-boats in the tonnage of enemy shipping sunk, though much of this would be lost to mines laid by these boats rather than torpedo attacks.

On 1 October 1941, Petersen was posted to the Admiralty Staff as Führer der Torpedoboote. Petersen returned to the E-boats on 20 April 1942 when he was appointed Führer der Schnellboote. It is also interesting to note that when the war badge issued to E-boat crews was redesigned in January 1943, Petersen was consulted and contributed his thoughts to the new design. On 13 June 1944, Petersen received the Oak-Leaves addition to his Knight's Cross in recognition of the continued high level of performance by units under his command. He was also only one of a tiny handful of expert E-boat commanders to receive the rare solid-silver version of the E-boat War Badge with diamond-studded swastika, a personal gift and token of esteem from the C-in-C Navy, Grossadmiral Raeder. He survived the war, a highly respected naval commander, and died in Flensburg, Schleswig-Holstein, in 1983.

Oberst Walter Oesau

Born on 28 June 1913 in Farnewinkel, Walter 'Gulle' Oesau started his military career with the Army, enlisting in the artillery in 1933. The promising young soldier transferred to the Luftwaffe where he was accepted by a transport unit before attending the military academy in Hannover. In 1934, as an officer candidate (Fahnenjunker), he completed basic flying training before being posted to Jagdgeschwader Richthofen as a freshly commissioned Leutnant. On the outbreak of the Spanish Civil War, Oesau was one of the first pilots to join Jagdstaffel 88 in Spain. Here he gained ace status, shooting down eight Republican aircraft, along with contemporaries such as Werner Mölders and Adolf Galland. He was also wounded in action for the first time. At the end of the conflict, Oesau became one of only 27 German servicemen to be awarded the rare Spanish Cross in Gold with Diamonds.

In July 1939, Oesau, now with the rank of Oberleutnant, became Staffelkapitän of 1/Jagdgeschwader 20. His first 'kill' of World War II came on 13 May 1940 during the campaign in the West, when he shot down a French 'Curtiss' fighter. By the end of the campaign, he had raised this to five, bringing his overall total to 13. With the air assault on England, his score began to rise steadily and between September 1939 and 18 August 1940 he shot down 20 enemy aircraft, an achievement that brought him the award of the Knight's Cross of the Iron Cross. Oesau continued to increase his tally over the coming months, and by 5 February 1941 had amassed 40 kills. The following day, he was awarded the Oak-Leaves for his Knight's Cross.

Following the invasion of the Soviet Union in 1941, Oesau and his squadron moved east. He found rich pickings here and by mid-July his score had risen to 80 kills, bringing him the coveted Swords addition, only the third recipient of this award. Shortly thereafter he was transferred to the Western Front to take command of Jagdgeschwader 2. Here his score continued to rise and by 26 October he had amassed 100 kills. At this stage he was ordered to give up combat flying and posted to a number of staff positions.

As the war progressed, attrition amongst fighter pilots meant that Oesau was recalled to combat duties. Now, as Kommodore of

Jagdgeschwader 1, he was to add to his skills in combating enemy fighters by becoming an 'expert' killer of four-engined bombers, shooting down 14 US heavy bombers, both B17 Flying Fortresses and B24 Liberators. On 11 May 1944, Oesau was leading a flight of Bf 109 G-6 aircraft to attack a formation of US bombers: his planes were attacked by an escorting force of P-38 'Lightning' fighters, and Oesau was shot down and killed, crashing near the town of St Vith. He had flown over 300 combat missions and achieved a total of 127 kills, 38 of which were Spitfires and 14 of which were four-engined bombers (or 'Viermots' as the German fighter pilots called them), which were notoriously difficult to take down.

Hauptmann Karl-Lothar Schulz

Schulz was born in Königsberg, East Prussia, on 30 April 1907. He joined the Army on leaving school and briefly served with an Artillery regiment, though his own personal training

Fighter ace Walter 'Gulle' Oesau is shown here posing by the nose of his Me 109 fighter. Oesau served with the Condor Legion during the Spanish Civil War, earning ace status there and winning the rare Spanish Cross in Gold with Diamonds, one of only 28 such awards. The latter is visible here on the right breast of his jerkin. (Josef Charita)

was as a pioneer. He joined the Police in 1925 and in 1933 was transferred to the newly formed Polizei Abteilung z.b.v. Wecke, the forerunner of the elite Hermann Göring Division. He was commissioned as a Police Lieutenant in 1934 and remained with the unit as it evolved into Landespolizeigruppe General Göring.

In September 1935 the unit was transferred into the Luftwaffe as Regiment General Göring. Göring decided that amongst his new elite troops would be a body of men trained as paratroopers. A call for volunteers went out, and Schulz was one of the first to come forward. He subsequently underwent paratrooper training and served as company commander of 15 (Pionier) Kompanie, a component of the parachute-trained IV.Bataillon/Regiment General Goring. In March 1938, a further re-organisation took place and IV.Bataillon was separated from the Regiment and became I.Bataillon of the newly formed

Oberst Karl-Lothar Schulz in November 1944. His Knight's Cross was decorated with Oak-Leaves with Swords for his part in events at Waalhaven airfield in May 1940. (Josef Charita)

Fallschirmjäger-Regiment 1. By 1940 Schulz had been promoted from company commander and was serving as commander of III.Battailon/Fallschirmjäger-Regiment 1.

During the campaign in the West, Schulz and his men dropped into Holland to seize the airport at Waalhaven near Rotterdam, in order to allow the rapid landing of more German troops. The airport was defended by a battalion of Dutch troops supported by a battery of 7.5cm guns, four armoured vehicles and a platoon of anti-aircraft gun crews. The Dutch defenders opened fire on the German paratroops as they descended but the Fallschirmjäger suffered only relatively light casualties. Shortly after the paratroopers had landed, elements of Infanterie-Regiment 16 arrived on the scene to give support, and with their help the Schulz-led paratroops secured the airfield. The Dutch were by no means finished, however, and gunboats were brought up to bombard the German positions. The RAF appeared too, and six light bombers attacked the German positions, before being driven off by the Luftwaffe with all but one of them shot down. A further Dutch counter-attack with armour and artillery support was also beaten off, and Schulz was able to send out a message giving the all clear for German aircraft to begin landing elements of 22 Air Landing Division. For the part played by the troops under his command in seizing and holding the vital airfield against strong enemy counter-attacks, Schulz was decorated with the Knight's Cross of the Iron Cross on 24 May 1940.

He was promoted to Major on 19 July 1940, took part in the invasion of Crete, and subsequently served with great distinction on the Eastern Front, first as a battalion then as a regimental commander. He was awarded the Oak-Leaves for his Knight's Cross on 20 April 1944 as Oberst in command of Fallschirmjäger-Regiment 1. Subsequently promoted to command 1.Fallschirm-Division, he fought in Italy on the Anzio/Nettuno bridgehead and at Monte Cassino. On 18 November he received the Swords addition to his Oak-Leaves. He was promoted to the rank of Generalmajor on 17 January 1945. Karl-Lothar Schulz died of natural causes in 1972.

Major Helmut Wick

Helmut Wick was born in Mannheim in the State of Baden on 5 August 1915. Living near an airfield, he developed a fascination for flying at an early age. His intended career in forestry work came to an end when he joined the Luftwaffe in 1936 at the age of 21. He successfully completed all of his training, and was commissioned as a Leutnant in 1938. It is interesting to note that his flying instructor at one stage was none other than future ace Werner Mölders.

1

2   3

4   5   6

7

8

A

'SILENT OTTO' KRETSCHMER
ON THE BRIDGE OF *U-99*
DURING A CONVOY ATTACK

B

FIGHTER ACE WALTER OESAU AFTER HIS 20TH 'KILL'

LUDWIG KEPPLINGER, THE FIRST WAFFEN-SS NCO KNIGHT'S CROSS WINNER

D

SS-UNTERSTURMFÜHRER FRITZ VOGT CAPTURES AN ENEMY COLUMN, FRANCE 1940

F

G

OBERLEUTNANT RUDOLF WITZIG IN THE ASSAULT ON EBEN EMAEL, 10 MAY 1940

Wick was posted to Jagdgeschwader Richthofen in 1939, but saw no part in the Polish campaign as his squadron was tasked with the defence of Berlin. In May 1940, the Geschwader was moved to the Western Front, and Wick soon began to make a name for himself as a first-rate pilot. Within a month of arriving at the front, he became the leading ace of the Richthofen Geschwader with a tally of 12 air victories, and was awarded the Iron Cross First Class. Success also brought him promotion to Staffelkapitän of 3. Staffel/Jagdgeschwader Richthofen. Many of Wick's early victories were obsolete French aircraft but with the start of the Battle of Britain, Wick found himself in constant action against RAF Spitfires and Hurricanes. His score continued to rise though, and on 27 August 1940, after scoring his 20th victory, he was awarded the Knight's Cross of the Iron Cross. By 5 October, he had more than doubled his tally, bringing him the Oak-Leaves addition and promotion to the rank of Major at the age of just 25 – the youngest in the Luftwaffe to hold this rank. On 28 November, Wick scored his 55th victory, giving him the lead over even the legendary greats like Galland (52) and Mölders (54).

That same day, he scored yet another victory in a high-altitude dogfight over the Isle of Wight, but during the course of the action, became separated from the other German pilots. He headed south for home in a long shallow dive. An RAF Spitfire had spotted him though, and attacked from the west with the sun behind. A hail of fire hit Wick's Messerschmitt as the Spitfire made an oblique pass, bullets ripping through his fuel tanks. Wick's controls were still responding but it was clear to him that the aircraft could not be saved. Another pass by the Spitfire saw the tail reduced to a shattered wreck. The joystick was jammed against his left leg as the aircraft, now out of control, began a series of spiralling stalls. The engine, starved of fuel, had stopped, producing an apprehensive silence as Wick struggled to reach the canopy release lever, leaving him helpless if the enemy decided to finish him off. Suddenly, the canopy released. Wick undid his harness and launched himself from the cockpit, seconds before the fumes from the ruptured fuel tanks ignited and blew the Messerschmitt apart. As he tumbled towards the cold waters of the English Channel, his wingman roared past, watching anxiously. His comrade was relieved to see Wick's parachute eventually open and lower him gently into the sea. It was, however, becoming darker and colder. There was little his wingman could do but return to base and report Wick's safe exit from his aircraft.

Wick was never found and is presumed to have drowned at sea. His rise to 'expert' status had been meteoric. In just over seven months he had gone from a novice pilot to being one of the top aces of his time, shooting down a total of 56 enemy aircraft.

This fine study of Helmut Wick shows him as a major after having received the Oak-Leaves for his Knight's Cross. The Oak-Leaves were awarded (and Wick was promoted from Hauptmann) a mere 39 days after the award of the Knight's Cross. Wick was the youngest major in the Luftwaffe at this time. (Josef Charita)

SS-Brigadeführer Fritz Witt

Fritz Witt was born on 27 May 1908 in Hohenlimburg. An early member of the SS, he was one of the original 120 founding members of the Leibstandarte-SS Adolf Hitler. He joined the Deutschland Regiment in 1935 and was still with this unit, serving as a company commander, when war broke out in 1939. During the Polish campaign, on 19 September 1939, he was decorated with the Iron Cross Second Class and this was followed quickly by the First Class, just six days later. Promoted to SS-Sturmbannführer and given command of I.Bataillon of the regiment, Witt led his troops with considerable élan during the campaign in the West, seeing fierce combat action in Holland and France, in particular the battles around the La Bassée Canal and on the Langres Plateau. In recognition of his spirited leadership of the battalion and its successes during the campaign, Witt was decorated with the Knight's Cross on 4 September 1940. Following the successful conclusion of the *Westfeldzug*, Witt returned to the Leibstandarte. An extremely popular officer with his troops, he was calm and composed even under heavy enemy fire, setting an example to his men. He received the Oak-Leaves addition to his Knight's Cross on 1 January 1943. At this point he held the rank of SS-Standartenführer and commanded SS-Panzer-grenadier-Regiment 1.

When the Hitlerjugend Division was formed in 1943, a cadre of the best officers and experienced NCOs and men from the Leibstandarte was transferred to provide the backbone of the new division. Witt was one of these officers and with the rank of SS-Brigadeführer und Generalmajor der Waffen-SS, was given command. The Hitlerjugend was thrown into the thick of the fighting around Caen during the battle for Normandy. On 16 June, Witt and his staff were relaxing and playing cards during a lull in the fighting when suddenly a barrage of large-calibre shells fired by Allied warships lying offshore crashed into the German positions. Witt and one of his junior officers were killed instantly. When he learned of the loss, Sepp Dietrich is reported to have said: 'That's one of the best gone. Witt was too good a soldier to survive for long.'

Oberst Werner Baumbach

Werner Baumbach was born on 27 December 1916 in the town of Cloppenburg. Fascinated by flying from an early age, as a young man he took up glider flying, a popular sport in Germany between the wars. He gained his glider pilot's licence, and then fulfilled his early ambitions by joining the Luftwaffe at the age of 19. He attended the Luftwaffe's Kriegsschule in Berlin-Gatow, and by the outbreak of war in 1939 was a commissioned officer and qualified pilot, flying bombers.

SS-Brigadeführer Fritz Witt was one of the most capable commanders in the Waffen-SS. It was no surprise that when the new 'Hitlerjugend' Panzer Division was formed and a cadre of the finest troops from the elite 'Leibstandarte' was transferred to form the core of this new division, Witt took command of this new unit. (Josef Charita)

One of the last photographs of Witt, taken in France in 1944 at the headquarters of the Hitlerjugend Division. Shortly afterwards, his Division would be thrown into the fighting for Caen, and Witt killed when his headquarters was shelled by British warships lying offshore. (Josef Charita)

During the Polish campaign, Baumbach was decorated with the Iron Cross Second Class for his part in an attack on a Polish airbase near Warsaw. Initially flying the Heinkel He III, shortly after the conclusion of the Polish campaign, Baumbach and his unit, Kampfgeschwader 30, changed to the Junkers Ju 88. Baumbach at this time was predominantly employed on anti-shipping strikes, including attacks on British warships and supply convoys during the invasion of Norway. On 4 May 1940, he was awarded the Iron Cross First Class. His flying and marksmanship skills soon paid dividends. His ultimate score on such missions was over 300,000 tons of shipping sunk, outstripping those of even the great U-boat aces. For his success in these missions, he was decorated with the Knight's Cross on 8 May 1940.

After the fall of France, Baumbach took part in the air assault on London. On one occasion his Ju 88 was badly shot up and only just made

Hauptmann Werner Baumbach
Träger des Eichenlaubs
zum Ritterkreuz des Eisernen Kreuzes

it back to Holland: he was forced to crash land, and ended up spending several months recuperating. His unit was subsequently moved north, and from bases in Norway continued to achieve considerable success against Allied shipping, especially after the German invasion of the Soviet Union in 1941 and the start of the shipping of 'lend-lease' material from Great Britain and the USA to the Soviet Union by convoy. Baumbach was awarded the Oak-Leaves for his Knight's Cross on 14 July 1941, only the 20th German soldier to be so honoured. The Swords followed on 17 August 1942, the 16th recipient of this addendum to the Oak-Leaves. Two months later he was promoted to Major.

Thereafter, Major Baumbach and his squadron moved to the Mediterranean front. Here his unit faced a total lack of organisation, due primarily to bureaucratic incompetence. Baumbach fired off a furious complaint direct to the Chief of the Luftwaffe General Staff, Generaloberst Jeschonnek. Göring ensured that things

Werner Baumbach is shown here as a Hauptmann, wearing the Knight's Cross with Oak-Leaves. He poses in full flight gear, in front of his Junkers Ju 88 A-4 bomber, the aircraft in which he achieved his greatest successes as an anti-shipping strike pilot.

were put right, but punished the young officer for bypassing the 'correct' communication channels by posting him into a backwater administrative post in a research establishment testing new radio-controlled bombs. Baumbach made strenuous personal efforts to ensure that a proposal to employ manned V1 rockets in a suicide role was thwarted, by appealing directly to Hitler who, agreeing with Baumbach, quashed the plans.

The outspoken young officer once again risked incurring Göring's wrath when, personally asked by Hitler for his opinion on the conduct of the air war, he gave a full, frank and extremely critical response. This time though, the Reichsmarschall avoided punishing him again and simply ignored his comments. Baumbach ended the war with the rank of Oberst. He suffered the indignity of having all of his decorations

Baumbach (on the right) is shown here with fellow aces Joachim Helbig (left) and Generalmajor Dietrich Peltz (centre), the officer in command of the bombing campaign against England. (Josef Charita)

This photograph shows Baumbach after the award of the Swords to his Oak-Leaves in August 1941. Baumbach surpassed the great U-boat aces in the tonnage of enemy shipping he sank.

looted, though they were later returned to him, and was questioned over allegations that aircraft of his unit had strafed survivors of sunk ships; but the allegations were proved groundless and he was released. He enjoyed a successful post-war career in aircraft development until his untimely death in an aircraft crash in October 1953.

Oberst Joachim Helbig

Joachim Helbig was born on 10 September 1915 in the town of Börln. Like several other Luftwaffe aces, the early part of his military career was actually spent in the Army: he was for a time an officer cadet in the artillery, serving with Artillerie-Regiment 4 in Dresden. He transferred to the Luftwaffe with the rank of Leutnant in 1936 and initially served as an observer (Beobachter) before going on to undertake flying training and becoming a pilot.

On the outbreak of war, Helbig served as an Oberleutnant with Lehrgeschwader 1 and flew missions during the Polish campaign. Only a few days after the opening of the campaign, he was involved in a motorcycle accident and missed the remainder, though in the following months he was involved in anti-shipping strikes against British vessels, flying the Heinkel He III. During this period he was awarded the Iron Cross Second Class. He subsequently saw service during the invasion of Norway, on one occasion having to use all his skills to nurse his badly damaged He III back to base with his crew badly wounded too: the nerve-wracking flight took two and a half hours. His unit was re-equipped with Junkers Ju 88 bombers, and during the assaults on France and the Low Countries he earned the Iron Cross First Class.

Helbig was a fearless combat pilot. On one occasion after a dive-bombing attack on a British warship, he engaged and despatched three Spitfires, throwing his large twin-engined bomber around like a tiny fighter. Despite serious damage to his aircraft, and his own serious wounds, he managed to return his aircraft safely to Düsseldorf: one of his crewmen bandaged his wounds as he piloted the aircraft. At the conclusion of the campaign in the West, Helbig was promoted to Hauptmann. On 13 August 1940, Helbig led his Staffel as part of II.Gruppe, Lehrgeschwader 1 on an attack on the British airfield at Worthy Down. Helbig's nine Ju 88s were flying at the end of the German formation, the position most likely to be attacked first. When the Germans did come under attack by some 80 Spitfires, Helbig's Staffel bore the brunt of the assault. The German formation was torn apart, and the skies filled with the parachutes of aircrew bailing out from their doomed aircraft. Soon, Helbig's aircraft was the sole survivor of the Staffel as his crew fought desperately to fend off attack after attack by enemy fighters. With his port engine shot up and his gunner and radio operator seriously wounded, Helbig headed back towards the Channel. As he edged out over the sea, believing he had reached safety, another Spitfire appeared on his tail – and Helbig awaited the coup de grace for his crippled bomber. But no attempt was made to attack. The British fighter flew 30m from the wingtip of the damaged Ju 88 all the way back across the Channel. As they approached the French coast, the Germans watched in amazement as the British pilot saluted, waggled his wings and set course back to England. Had the British pilot shown chivalrous respect to a wounded enemy, or had he simply run out of ammunition? Helbig was the only pilot of his Staffel to return, and he subsequently undertook many more attacks, both day and night, on targets in England. On 24 November 1940, after completing a total of 75 combat missions, he was decorated with the Knight's Cross. Whereas fighter pilots were usually granted the award based on the number of enemy aircraft shot down, bomber pilots were normally cited for the number of combat missions flown. Helbig was then transferred to the Mediterranean theatre where he took part in the air assault on Malta. By January 1942, his total of combat missions flown had reached 300, and on the 16th of that month he became the 64th soldier to receive the Oak-Leaves addition to the Knight's Cross.

Helbig and his crews were part of the elite band of German airmen who became personally known to the enemy: the British called his squadron 'The Helbig Flyers'. He was also extremely proficient in attacking enemy shipping and during his stint of duty in the Mediterranean his squadron sank three British destroyers. The British made determined efforts to put Helbig's squadron out of action, even resorting to a commando

Major Joachim Helbig, leader of the squadron which became notorious to RAF pilots as 'The Helbig Flyers'. Helbig was a superb pilot, and like his comrade in arms Baumbach achieved such a tally of enemy ships sunk that it placed him alongside the great U-boat aces. (Josef Charita)

raid in July 1942, when many of his aircraft were destroyed on the ground. As soon as replacement aircraft arrived, Helbig was back in action again, and by 28 September 1942, he had amassed an astonishing 500 combat missions and 200,000 tons of enemy shipping sunk, earning him the Swords to his Oak-Leaves, the 20th recipient of the award, along with promotion to the rank of Major. Two months later, during an attack on an Allied convoy, Helbig destroyed a 10,000-ton ammunition ship, bringing his own personal score of enemy shipping sunk to 180,000 tons.

As already witnessed, it was common practice for the top aces across all branches to be transferred to non-combat duties, in order to avoid damage to German morale should they be killed in action, and to ensure that their immense practical combat experience could be passed on by using them to coach and train the next generation of potential aces. Helbig's break from combat was not long, however, and by 1944 pilot attrition forced his return to combat duty. He took an active part in the defence of the Anzio/Nettuno and Normandy fronts. Helbig survived the war, and died in an automobile accident in Spain in October 1965.

Oberst Günther Lützow

Günther Lützow was born in Kiel on 4 September 1912. Despite being a student of theology, he was drawn to a military career – hardly surprising given that he came from one of Germany's most famous families with a centuries-old military tradition. An early volunteer for the Luftwaffe, Lützow served in the Condor Legion during the Spanish Civil War where he honed his flying skills to perfection and gained ace status by shooting down five enemy aircraft. He earned himself the Spanish Cross in Gold.

On returning to Germany, he became an instructor at the Fighter Pilot School, passing on his own skills to fledgling pilots. By the outbreak of World War II, Lützow was serving with Jagdgeschwader 3 Udet, becoming Geschwader-kommodore in August 1940. On 18 September 1940, during the Battle of Britain, he shot down his 15th enemy aircraft, bringing him the award of the Knight's Cross of the Iron Cross. He gradually increased his tally, and by the time his Geschwader moved eastwards for Operation BARBAROSSA in the summer of 1941, he had shot down 40 enemy aircraft. On 20 July he was awarded the Oak-Leaves addition to his Knight's Cross, the 27th soldier to receive this. BARBAROSSA marked the start of a rapid increase in combat victories for Lützow. By 11 October, just 76 days later, he had more than doubled his score, to 92 enemy aircraft destroyed. During that same month, he became only the second fighter pilot in the entire Luftwaffe to reach a score of 100 enemy aircraft shot down. Once again, success

Günther Lützow was one of Germany's finest fighter pilots, and was only one of a small number of Luftwaffe aces who achieved kills with a jet fighter. He is shown here after the award of the Swords to his Oak-Leaves in October 1941. Lützow was only the second Luftwaffe fighter pilot to achieve a score of 100 enemy aircraft shot down. (Josef Charita)

Günther Lützow spoke his mind freely: his furious reaction to Hermann Göring's criticism of the bravery of his fighter pilots saw him threatened with court martial. Lützow served in JV44, the so-called 'Squadron of Experts' under Generalleutnant Adolf Galland. Lützow was another of those who sat for a portrait by the famed war artist Willrich (*right*). Although perhaps not particularly flattering, it captures Lützow's steely-eyed determination. (Josef Charita)

brought with it a recall from combat duties, and Lützow went on to fill a number of administrative posts, ending up as a Jagdfliegerführer, or Fighter Leader.

In January 1945, during a conference called by Reichsmarschall Göring, Lützow had a frank exchange with his commander-in-chief, criticising Göring's failure to support his pilots, his offensive remarks about some pilots being cowards, the conduct of the war in general, and the sacking of Adolf Galland as General of the Fighters. The enraged Reichsmarschall threatened to have Lützow court-martialled, but failed to carry through his threat. Instead Lützow was posted to Italy as Jagdfliegerführer – as far from Berlin and Göring as possible.

In the closing days of the war, Lützow returned to combat sorties, operating the Me 262 jet fighter in Jagdverband 44, the so-called 'Squadron of Experts' commanded by the now-recalled Galland. The majority of pilots in this squadron were high-ranking, decorated fighter aces. Lützow was able to score two more kills before being reported missing in action on 24 April 1945. Despite his long absence from combat due to various staff appointments, he clocked up over 300 combat missions and achieved 108 victories. Lützow was a man of integrity and moral fortitude who despised the political hierarchy and military bureaucracy and spoke his mind, despite the dangers of so doing in the Third Reich. No doubt his earlier theological training did much to form his character. He was universally admired and respected by his peers and is often described as embodying all that was decent and honourable about the German military character.

SS-Sturmbannführer Ludwig Kepplinger

Ludwig Kepplinger, an Austrian, was born in Linz in December 1911 and originally served with the Austrian Mountain Troops. Thrown out of the Army for espousing his right-wing political beliefs, he moved to Bavaria and in 1935, volunteered for the SS-Verfügungstruppe. He originally served with the Deutschland Regiment but returned to his native Austria in 1938 on the founding of the new Der Führer Regiment in Vienna.

Kepplinger worked his way through the ranks, becoming an SS-Hauptscharführer by the outbreak of war in September 1939. During the campaign in the West, he served as a squad leader with an assault group from 11.Kompanie of the Regiment. On 10 May, Kepplinger and his men attacked the Dutch fort at Westervoort commanding the bridge over the River Issel. Having marched over 18km to reach their objective, they found the bridge had been blown. Undaunted, Kepplinger and two of his men crossed over the tangled wreckage of the bridge and launched a furious attack on the enemy positions with hand grenades. Overcome by the ferocity of the attack, over 90 soldiers of the Dutch garrison surrendered. Thirty more prisoners were captured later on the same day. Then, acting on his own while his comrades guarded the prisoners, Kepplinger attacked further Dutch bunkers with more hand grenades, swiftly neutralising enemy fire. Kepplinger's good fortune ran out the following day when he received multiple bullet wounds and was hospitalised. Whilst recovering he learned that he had been decorated with both Second and First Class Iron Crosses. Kepplinger's action, leading a force of only three men including himself to neutralise a key enemy strongpoint, had ensured the rapid progress

Ludwig Kepplinger is shown here in his field grey service uniform as an SS-Hauptscharführer with the SS-Verfügungs-Division, the forerunner of the famous Das Reich Division. (Josef Charita)

49

A Willrich portrait of Kepplinger, showing him in the combat clothing worn at the time of his Knight's Cross winning action, with camouflage smock and steel helmet. He is armed with the MP28, a popular sub-machine gun and forerunner of the mass-produced MP38/40. (Josef Charita)

RIGHT **Kepplinger after his commissioning, whilst serving as an SS-Sturmbannführer and commander of the Panzer-Abteilung of 17.SS-Panzer-grenadier-Division Götz von Berlichingen. Kepplinger was killed whilst riding as a passenger in a vehicle that came under enemy fire in Normandy in September 1944.**

of his Regiment. His superiors had only authorised the two lower classes of the Iron Cross to ensure that their subsequent recommendation for the Knight's Cross, of which he was unaware, would be swiftly approved. Kepplinger was awarded this on 4 September 1940, the first NCO in the Waffen-SS to be so decorated. This was followed by a battlefield commission to the rank of SS-Untersturmführer and a posting to the elite Wiking Division.

Kepplinger subsequently rose to the rank of SS-Sturmbannführer and commanded SS-Panzer-Abteilung 17, in the Götz von Berlichingen Division. On 6 August 1944, during the fighting in Normandy, Kepplinger was in charge of a number of stragglers who had gathered at an assembly point for regrouping. These were predominantly Panzer soldiers, like Kepplinger, whose vehicles had been knocked out. On their way back to the front, the truck in which they were travelling came under a hail of enemy fire. Kepplinger, who was sitting 'up front' with the driver, died instantly from a bullet to the head.

SS-Gruppenführer Heinz Reinefarth

Heinz Reinefarth was born in Gnesen in the district of Posnan, West Prussia, on 26 December 1903. A lawyer by profession, he joined the Allgemeine-SS, serving in its legal department: he reached the rank of SS-Hauptsturmführer (equivalent to a captain) before mobilisation of the German Army saw him called up for military service. Despite his commissioned rank in the SS, he was taken into the Army as an NCO and served with Infanterie-Regiment 337, part of 208.Infanterie-Division, winning the Iron Cross Second Class during the Polish campaign and the First Class on 28 May 1940 during the campaign in the West. On 25 June 1940, Feldwebel Reinefarth was decorated with the Knight's Cross of the Iron Cross.

After the successful conclusion of the campaign in the West, Reinefarth was demobilised and joined the Ordnungspolizei, the police administrative service, rising rapidly through the ranks. He served in occupied Bohemia-Moravia as Inspector of General Administration from June 1942 to June 1943, reaching the rank of Brigadeführer und Generalmajor der Polizei. From June to December 1943, he served in various administrative capacities at the Hauptamt Ordnungspolizei in Berlin. He was mobilised again in 1944, this time into the Waffen-SS (the Reichsführer-SS Heinrich Himmler was also endowed with the title of Chef der Deutschen Polizei). In August 1944 he was promoted to SS-Gruppenführer unde General-leutnant der Polizei. Reinefarth commanded a Kampfgruppe, serving under the Hohere SS-und Polizei Führer, Erich von dem Bach-Zelewski, during the suppression of the Warsaw Uprising. Despite his own distinguished conduct during the French campaign, Reinefarth was not a good commander at this level and troops under his command behaved with considerable barbarity during these operations. Despite his less than impressive performance, Oak-Leaves were added to Reinfarth's Knight's Cross on 30 September, for his part in the suppression of the Warsaw Uprising.

In December 1944 he was appointed as commander of XVIII SS-Armeekorps and commanded the fortress area of Küstrin on the Oder Front. His final post was as commander of XIV SS-Armee-Korps. He was captured by the British at the end of the war, and despite demands for his extradition by the Poles, he was exonerated at the end of his trial. He entered politics, becoming a member of the parliament of Schleswig-Holstein in 1958. No charges were ever brought against him for the atrocities committed by troops under his command, and he died in retirement in 1979.

Heinz Reinefarth rose from the ranks of a humble Feldwebel with the Army to become an SS-Gruppenführer and Generalmajor of the Police. Despite the personal bravery he had displayed in his early military career, he is better known for the atrocities of the security troops under his command in Poland in 1944. (Josef Charita)

SS-Obergruppenführer Felix Steiner

Felix Steiner was born in Ebenrode on 23 May 1896. He served as an Army officer during World War I, winning both the Second Class and First Class Iron Cross. By the end of hostilities in 1918 he had reached the rank of Oberleutnant. Demobbed after the end of the war, he returned to military service in 1921, serving with Infanterie-Regiment 1 of the Weimar Republic's Reichswehr, based in Königsberg. The following year, Steiner was appointed to the General Staff where he served in various posts until 1927; he was then promoted to Hauptmann, and returned to Infanterie-Regiment 1 as the Regimental Adjutant. In 1932 he was appointed as a company commander within the regiment.

In 1933, Steiner was given the task of training members of the Landespolizei to form the new Kasernierte Polizei (or Barracked Police), units formed on military lines and intended for possible future use as reinforcements on mobilisation of the Army during war. In 1935, Steiner volunteered for the SS-Verfügungstruppe and was accepted into SS-Standarte Deutschland in Ellwangen as commander of III.Bataillon. By the following year, he had been promoted to SS-Standartenführer and given command of the Regiment. Steiner fostered close links with the pocket battleship of the same name, Panzerschiff *Deutschland*.

The Regiment took part in the Anschluss with Austria under Steiner's command, and on the invasion of Poland was attached to Panzer

Felix Steiner was an extremely popular and well-respected commander. Note that in this photo he does not wear the collar patches of his rank. Senior ranking officers would not normally remove such insignia: their omission indicates that they made the wearer an easy target for enemy snipers. (Josef Charita)

OPPOSITE BELOW **A smiling Steiner, now an SS-Obergruppenführer, chats with his men. Steiner showed great concern for the welfare of his men. When Hitler ordered him to attack towards Berlin with his remaining troops in the closing days of the war, Steiner, knowing the futility of the mission and the pointless loss of life that would ensue, simply ignored the command. (Josef Charita)**

A fine portrait of Steiner as an SS-Gruppenführer, wearing the Oak-Leaves on his Knight's Cross. The white enamelled cross worn below the Knight's Cross is a Finnish campaign decoration. (Josef Charita)

Division 'Kempf', supporting Panzer-Regiment 7. Steiner's SS troops took part in the crossing of the Narew at Roshan, advancing to the Bug at Brok and the attack on the fortress at Deplin on the Vistula. Steiner's greatest accomplishment was his participation in the capture of the Polish fortress at Modlin on 28 September 1939, when 1,200 enemy officers, 24,000 NCOs and men, 5,000 horses, 105 artillery pieces, 80 mortars, 370 machine guns and over 13,000 small arms were seized, all for the loss of just 15 SS troops killed and 35 wounded. Steiner was awarded the Clasps to both his Second and First Class Iron Crosses for these achievements.

Following the successful conclusion of the Polish campaign, Deutschland, together with the Der Führer and Germania regiments, and numerous other smaller units, were brought together to form the SS-Verfügungs-Division. During the attack on France and the Low Countries in 1940, Steiner's SS troops fought with the same determination they had shown in Poland, sweeping aside opposition as they crossed the Kleve; pushed through Kronenburg, Tilburg and Breda; took the islands of Seeland, Vlissingen and Beveland; broke through the Weygand Line; and penetrated deep behind enemy lines. For his inspired command of the Regiment during the Polish and Western campaigns, Steiner was decorated with the Knight's Cross on 15 August 1940.

On 1 December 1940, as a newly promoted SS-Brigadeführer, he was appointed to command the new Wiking Division. Under Steiner's command, Wiking became one of the most highly respected Waffen-SS divisions, even earning the grudging respect of several of the senior commanders of the Red Army who faced it in battle. He commanded this elite division with considerable skill, earning the Oak-Leaves addition to his Knight's Cross on 23 December 1942, and the Swords on 10 August 1944 for his command of III.(germanisches) Panzer-Korps. Steiner's troops, often referred to as the 'European-SS', largely comprised Germanic volunteers from Holland, Denmark and Sweden.

In the closing days of the war, Steiner's troops were ordered by Hitler to

attempt break through the Soviet encirclement of Berlin. Steiner was well aware of the futility of such an action and refused to sacrifice the lives of his remaining troops in such a pointless operation. He survived the war and died in retirement in Munich at the age of 70 in 1966.

Oberarzt Dr Rolf Karl Ernst Jäger

Rolf Jäger was born in Klein Kunterstein in the Graudenz on 1 November 1912. He joined the military on 15 September 1934 when he enlisted into the First Aid section of 6.Infanterie-Division of the Reichsheer. In November of that year he attended the Military Medical Academy in Berlin, and one year later transferred to the Luftwaffe.

After briefly attending the Ariel Warfare School at Berlin-Gatow, he transferred to the Luftwaffe Sports School where his medical training continued. In January 1937 he was promoted to the rank of Unterarzt, a medical corps rank equivalent to that of Leutnant, whereupon he was posted to Luftgau VI in Münster. Promotion to Arzt (Oberleutnant) followed in December 1928 and to Oberarzt (Hauptmann) in February 1939.

Jäger was posted to Fallschirm-Sturm-Bataillon Koch during preparations for the campaign in the West. He took part in the attack on the bridges over the Albert Canal in Belgium, being landed along with the battalion staff element near Vroenhoven. As soon as he arrived, Jäger began tending to the numerous wounded and injured paratroopers. Along with other medics he personally recovered the bodies of seven of his fallen comrades and recovered 24 wounded men whilst under heavy enemy fire, ignoring the severe risk to his own life. Such devotion to the welfare of his injured comrades did not go unnoticed and on 12 May 1940 he was awarded the Iron Cross Second Class. This, however, was merely to fulfil the first required stage before the Knight's Cross bestowal. The Iron Cross First Class followed on 13 May, and on 15 May Oberarzt Dr Jäger was awarded the Knight's Cross of the Iron Cross for conspicuous gallantry in tending Fallschirmjäger wounded whilst under heavy enemy fire. This great distinction was followed just five days later by promotion to Stabsarzt (Major).

Jäger's distinguished career was to continue through many more campaigns. He served during the invasion of Crete, on the Eastern Front (where Jäger was promoted to Oberstabsarzt/Oberstleutnant) and in Italy during the Allied landings at Anzio and Nettuno. He was always in the forefront of care for the wounded. Jäger was ultimately appointed to command the Military Hospital at Tarvis in the north of Italy. When the war ended, Jäger entered British captivity. He returned to civilian life in 1947 after his discharge as a prisoner of war, and died in retirement in 1984. Jäger was one of only a small number of medical officers to be decorated with Germany's premier award for combat gallantry.

Dr Rolf Jäger was a member of an elite group – medical officers who were decorated with Germany's highest award for gallantry under fire.
(Josef Charita)

SS-Sturmbannführer Fritz Vogt

Fritz Vogt was born in Munich in March 1918. He volunteered for service in the SS-Verfügungstruppe in 1935 and was accepted into the Deutschland Regiment. As with all SS officers, a period of service in the ranks was required before a career as a commissioned officer could be considered, but shortly after he completed his training, he was selected as a potential officer and was eventually sent to the SS-Junkerschule in Braunschweig from which he graduated with the rank of SS-Untersturmführer in April 1939.

Vogt saw action as commander of a motorcycle reconnaissance platoon during the Polish campaign and distinguished himself by becoming the first man in his unit to win the Iron Cross Second Class. His regiment, as part of the SS-Verfügungs-Division, saw heavy combat during the attack on France and the Low Countries. Vogt's reconnaissance platoon was used as an assault group during an attack on Kleve in Holland in May 1940. His unit was tasked with securing a bridge that lay on the Division's line of advance and the attack was led from the front by Vogt himself. Ignoring fire from several heavily defended bunkers, Vogt and his men stormed the first of the enemy positions, without major injury. Using grenades, one enemy bunker after another was cleared. Eight in all fell, until the remaining Dutch troops surrendered, astonished by the ferocity of the attack. The enemy positions were seized and over 200 prisoners were taken, for the loss of just two Waffen-SS soldiers killed and with a few, including Vogt, suffering minor wounds. Vogt's was the only assault team in the area that day which achieved total success in its mission.

Soon afterwards, during the advance through Flanders, Vogt once again displayed the daring aggression for which he became known. His reconnaissance unit spotted a battalion-sized French column heading towards the main German force, clearly intent on counter-attacking. Vogt went into action immediately. His motorcycle troops, supported by two armoured cars, smashed headlong into the front of the enemy column, taking it completely by surprise. An anti-tank gun had meanwhile been designated to remain in its original position and open fire on the rear of the enemy column while Vogt attacked the front. Overwhelmed by the sheer aggressive energy of the attack, the French quickly surrendered. Vogt's small unit, comprising just 30 Waffen-SS troops, took 650 enemy prisoners.

On 7 June, Vogt's platoon came across a retreating French infantry column near Vrely and quickly overcame resistance with a display of

Fritz Vogt, shown here as an SS-Hauptsturmführer, was typical of the officer the Waffen-SS sought to create: bold, aggressive, fearless, and prepared to take on superior enemy forces without hesitation. Several of the most successful young officers of the Waffen-SS served, like Vogt, in the Aufklärungsabteilung (reconnaissance detachment) of their divisions. (Josef Charita)

A war artist's rendition of Vogt at the time of his Knight's Cross winning exploits in France in May 1940. Officers like Vogt wore the same camouflage combat kit as the men they commanded. Note also the stick grenades tucked into his belt. (Josef Charita)

sheer aggression. After a brief but heavy exchange of fire, the French surrendered and a further 250 enemy soldiers and two artillery pieces were added to Vogt's tally for the campaign so far. An award of the Iron Cross First Class was immediately authorised, but as news of his exploits during the campaign were collated at Divisional Headquarters, it became clear that something more than this was called for. On 4 September 1940, he was decorated with the Knight's Cross of the Iron Cross.

During the campaign on the Eastern Front, Vogt continued to show the same levels of daring and élan. On 1 July 1941, after a 27km march, he captured the enemy-held bridge at Pochowiece, holding it against determined counter-attacks. After being laid low by typhus, Vogt was posted as an instructor at various training schools before returning to the front, at his own request, at the end of 1943. He saw fierce action on the Leningrad Front at the Wolchow Bridgehead with the Norge Regiment. At the end of 1944, Vogt's unit was attached to the Wiking Division and in January 1945 was tasked with forcing a passage through to the encircled IX SS-Gebirgs-Korps in Budapest. His force was halted at the old castle at Gutes Hegyiks where they came under attack from enemy forces. For three solid days Vogt's men were engaged in bloody hand-to-hand fighting. When the Germans finally regrouped and tried to begin their advance, they came under attack from a strong force of enemy tanks. Vogt himself single-handedly destroyed three enemy tanks, his personal example of gallantry and determination providing great inspiration to his men. His unit eliminated 54 out of a total of 200 enemy tanks destroyed during this engagement. For his part in this battle, Vogt was decorated with the Oak-Leaves to his Knight's Cross on 16 March 1945.

Due to the chaos reigning at this late stage of the war, Vogt never received his own oak-leaf clasp. Only a few days later he was mortally wounded when his field car was strafed by enemy aircraft. His own commander, Karl Ullrich, took off his own oak-leaves and hung them around Vogt's neck, determined to ensure his dying comrade received the honour he was due.

Oberleutnant Rudolf Witzig

Witzig was born in Rohlinghausen on 14 August 1916. His military career began as an officer cadet with the Army's Pionier-Battailon 16 in 1935, and in 1937 he was commissioned as a Leutnant. He remained with the engineers for just ten more months before volunteering to transfer to the paratroops. In August 1938 he joined the Fallschirm-Infanterie-Bataillon and by October was a fully qualified paratrooper, entitled to wear the Army Paratrooper Badge. Two months later Witzig and all his comrades in the Fallschirm-Infanterie-Bataillon found themselves transferred to the

Luftwaffe, where Witzig continued as a combat engineer. In July 1939 he was promoted to Oberleutnant and shortly after the outbreak of war was given command of the Pionierezug of Fallschirm-Sturm-Abteilung Koch.

By April 1940, Witzig was commander of 17.Kompanie, Fallschirmjäger-Regiment 1. During the attack on France and the Low Countries it had been decided to drop paratroops ahead of the main invasion force to seize key targets such as bridges and defensive installations. One such target was the Eben Emael fortress, on the Belgian border. This massive structure

Willrich's portrait of Witzig, dressed in full combat clothing and with his MP38/40 slung over his shoulder. Note at top left the flaming comet emblem of the Fallschirm-Sturm-Regiment. (Josef Charita)

protected the Albert Canal, with its 6ft-thick concrete walls and its two 120mm and sixteen 75mm guns. It constituted a serious threat to the German advance, and needed to be neutralised. A plan for an attack on the fortress was produced by General Kurt Student in which Fallschirmjäger would seize the fort, as well as bridges at Veldvezelt, Vroenhoven and Canne, in a surprise attack. Oberleutnant Witzig, with the Pionier-Kompanie of II/Fallschirmjäger Regiment 1, would form assault group 'Granite' and have the daunting task of neutralising the fortress.

On 10 May 1940, the Fallschirmpioniere landed on the roof of the fortress by glider, but without their commander, who had been forced to abort his own flight due to problems with his glider and had returned to base to pick up new transport. Meanwhile his troops had stormed the fortress using flame-throwers and specially prepared powerful demolition charges. Within minutes a significant number of enemy guns had been put out of action by dropping explosive charges down the barrels, and the exit doors to the fortress blown open. When Witzig finally arrived three hours later, his troops had forced their way into the fortress exit but had made little further progress. By now the defenders had rallied and were putting up a stout defence of their positions: they had in fact called down their own artillery fire upon the fortress, hoping to wipe out the enemy. The Germans were forced to spend the night in the gun casemates they had captured. At daybreak reinforcements arrived and Witzig, determined to force the issue, led his men in an all-out assault. The ferocity of the renewed German attack was enough to dishearten the defenders, who hoisted a white flag and offered their surrender. Witzig, with a mere 85 men, had captured one of the world's most powerful and modern fortresses, together with its garrison of over 1,200 men for the loss of just six killed and twenty wounded. Witzig was immediately recommended for the award of the Knight's Cross, and Hitler swiftly approved. The only problem was that Witzig did not yet hold the Iron Cross Second or First Class, prerequisites for the award of the Knight's Cross. The solution was simple: Witzig was also awarded the two lower grades, thereby satisfying the award criteria. Every soldier involved in the attack was also advanced by one rank, resulting in Witzig being promoted to Hauptmann.

Witzig subsequently saw action in the airborne assault on Crete, in North Africa and on the Eastern Front where, on 25 November 1944, by then a Major, he was decorated with the Oak-Leaves addition to his Knight's Cross as commander of I/Fallschirm-Pionier-Regiment 21. He ended the war on the Western Front, being decorated also with the Roll of Honour Clasp of the Luftwaffe in May 1945. After the war, Witzig returned to military life once again with the West German Bundeswehr, reaching the rank of Oberst and serving on the staff of the

Pionierschule. When he finally retired in 1974, he had given 28 years of his life to the service of his country.

Major Ludwig Stautner

Ludwig Stautner was an experienced combat veteran of World War I. In September 1916, as a junior NCO with the rank of Vizefeldwebel serving with 1/Bayerisches-Jäger-Bataillon 6, he had been decorated with the Golden Bavarian Military Merit Medal for taking a French emplacement at Thiaumont and eleminating the enemy machine-gun position there. He was commissioned Leutnant der Reserve in February 1918.

Mountain troop commander Oberst Ludwig Stautner. Mountain troops were readily identified by the edelweiss sleeve badge, also worn as a metal emblem on the left side of their cap. The decorations worn by Stautner include several from his service in World War I. On his right breast pocket is the special insignia of an expert mountaineer. (Josef Charita)

This photograph, taken during the campaign at Narvik, shows the extremely inhospitable nature of the terrain, with very little cover to provide shelter from the elements. As can be seen here, every available man was pressed into service as infantry, including sailors whose ships had been sunk.

On the outbreak of World War II, Stautner was serving as a Battalion Commander in 3.Gebirgs-Division. Formed in 1938 from the amalgamation of 5 and 7 divisions of the Austrian Army on the Anschluss with Germany, the Division had taken part in the Polish campaign and served briefly in the campaign against France and the Low Countries before being chosen to lead the attack on the Norwegian post of Narvik. Stautner's regiment, Gebirgsjäger-Regiment 139, was transported to Narvik by sea aboard a fleet of German destroyers. It was a rather rough sea journey, which laid many of the mountain troopers low with violent seasickness.

Stautner led his battalion ashore at Bjervik. Although the town was taken with virtually no opposition, surprise attacks by Royal Navy warships decimated the German destroyer force leaving the mountain troopers stranded with no support. As many weapons as possible were unshipped from the wrecked destroyers and their crews were pressed into service on land. Stautner's 1.Bataillon, supported by a naval detachment, occupied an isolated series of trenches in the defence line to the north of Romboks Fjord.

The German defensive lines soon came under heavy pressure from Allied attacks. The area defended by Stautner's battalion was infiltrated during a blizzard by Norwegian troops wearing snow camouflage. In battalion strength and supported by artillery, the enemy troops posed a considerable threat. The Norwegians, however, were having difficulty manoeuvring their artillery through the snow, and on the following morning a Kampfgruppe from Stautner's battalion, wading chest deep through the snow, moved into position and covered by their heavy machine guns, attacked and eliminated the Norwegian unit. Despite such isolated successes, Allied pressure began to tell and the German perimeter was gradually constricted, with Stautner's battalion covering the northern sector. The town of Narvik itself was re-occupied on 27 May by sea-landed Allied troops, but only after fierce hand-to-hand fighting in some areas.

Allied attacks intensified and Stautner's troops took heavy punishment, but doggedly defended their rapidly shrinking perimeter. On 7 June an expected Allied attack on Stautner's positions began, but was nowhere near as heavy as anticipated and was easily fended off by the now greatly understrength battalion. Then, on the following day, patrols reported that enemy troops had evacuated Narvik. Just as it seemed the coup de grace was about to be delivered on the beleaguered mountain troopers, the enemy had decided to withdraw. For his part in the steadfast defence of the German perimeter at Narvik, the award of the Knight's Cross of the Iron Cross was authorised for Major Stautner on 20 June 1940.

GLOSSARY

Am Halse Worn at the neck.
Befurwortet Literally, 'Approved' – for the award of the Knight's Cross.
Eichenlaub Oak-Leaves.
Eichenlaub, Schwerter und Brillanten Oak-Leaves with Swords and Diamonds.
Eichenlaub und Schwertern Oak-Leaves with Swords.
Fraktur Gothic script.
Latein Latin script.
Oberkommando der Wehrmacht Armed Forces High Command.
Ritterkreuz Knight's Cross.
Ritterkreuz des Eisernen Kreuzes Knight's Cross of the Iron Cross.
Ritterkreuzträger Knight's Cross Bearer.
Ritterkreuzurkunde Formal award document for the Knight's Cross.
Soldbuch Soldier's ID book.
Vorläufiges Besitzzeugnis A preliminary certificate of possession following the award of the Cross.
Vorschlag A recommendation for the award of the Knight's Cross.
Wehrpass A soldier's military pass.

COLOUR PLATE COMMENTARY

A: THE IRON CROSS, KNIGHT'S CROSS AND AWARD DOCUMENTS

The medals shown represent the Iron Cross series of awards as re-instituted in September 1939. The Oak-Leaves, Oak-Leaves with Swords etc. were later additions. (1) is the Grand Cross and (2) is the Knight's Cross. (3) is the Iron Cross Second Class and (4) is the pin-back Iron Cross First Class. (5) is the 1939 Clasp for the 1914 Iron Cross First Class and (6) is the 1939 Clasp for the 1914 Iron Cross Second Class.

(7) is an example of the preliminary certificate of possession for the Knight's Cross. This simple pre-printed document had the recipient's name and rank, and the date and place of award, typed into the relevant blank spaces. The awarding authority then signed the document and the ink stamp was applied to the lower left corner. The signature on this particular document is that of Kapitän zur See Ehrhardt on the staff of the Naval Personnel Department in Berlin. (8) is a fine example of a Knight's Cross formal award document, granted to Oberjäger Johann Sandner. The fine calligraphy on this large, hand-made parchment vellum is mostly executed in dark brown ink, but the recipient's name and rank appear in gold leaf. This document was photographed in 1941 before completion and has not yet been signed, but will bear Hitler's signature at the foot. On the inside rear cover of the leather folder containing the vellum, the name of the artisan responsible for the binding (Frieda Thiersch) can usually be found, impressed in gold letters.

B: 'SILENT OTTO' KRETSCHMER ON THE BRIDGE OF *U-99* DURING A CONVOY ATTACK

Kapitänleutnant Otto Kretschmer, known to his men as 'Silent Otto', pioneered the concept of attacking from within the convoy itself rather than standing off and firing a torpedo into the mass of ships. Many of the great U-boat aces were boisterous characters but Kretschmer was, as his nickname suggests, much more reserved. Unlike many aces, he insisted his men keep themselves tidy and clean-shaven, using the highly unpopular special soap adapted for seawater. Kretschmer acquired for his crew a supply of captured lightweight British battledress blouses, which became so popular amongst U-boat crews that the Germans produced an almost exact copy of their own. During an inspection of his crew after a successful war cruise, Grossadmiral Raeder complimented him on the smart appearance of his men – not realising they were wearing enemy uniforms!

Kretschmer is shown at the attack binocular (*Überwasserzieloptik*) guiding the boat into position as he prepares to finish off an enemy freighter, bringing his total tonnage sunk to 50,000, and with this the award of the Knight's Cross. Although his career was cut short by the sinking of his boat and his capture, the high level of enemy shipping he sank ensured him a place in history as one of the great U-boat aces. He was accorded considerable respect by the Allies after his capture and went on to reach high rank in the post-war Federal German Navy.

C: FIGHTER ACE WALTER OESAU AFTER HIS 20TH 'KILL'

Walter 'Gulle' Oesau is shown here describing how he has just shot down an RAF Hurricane fighter, to a squadron comrade. This kill has raised his score to the then requisite '20 kills', which makes him eligible for the Knight's Cross. This award level was greatly increased as the war lengthened. He wears flight gear, including a lightweight pilot's jerkin (one of many different variants of this style of clothing) on which is pinned (on his right breast) the diamond-studded Spanish Cross in Gold he won with the Condor Legion during the Civil War in Spain. He also wears (on his left side) the special version of the wound badge instituted in 1936 to recognise those wounded in action in Spain, and the Iron Cross First Class.

His aircraft at this time was a Messerschmitt Bf 109E. This version of the Me 109 was faster than the Spitfire and Hurricane it opposed, but had a larger turning circle, which meant that slower aircraft could often outmanoeuvre it. The Me 109 was also relatively heavily armed, carrying a 2cm cannon firing through the propeller boss as well as two machine guns on the engine cowling and two in the wings. All in all, the main fighter aircraft of the RAF and Luftwaffe were reasonably well matched, with the outcome of a dogfight very much dependent on the skills of the individual pilots.

D: LUDWIG KEPPLINGER, THE FIRST WAFFEN-SS NCO KNIGHT'S CROSS WINNER

Kepplinger was awarded the Knight's Cross for his bravery in attacking an enemy bunker, part of the Grebbe defence line, on his own. Finding the bridge that was his primary objective blown, he and his men stormed over the tangled remains and attacked the enemy positions on the opposite bank. Kepplinger then attacked the enemy bunker with a machine pistol and hand grenades. He is shown here (at centre) in the aftermath of this action, seriously wounded, being helped away by comrades: he has been shot several times – once in the hand, twice in the upper thigh and twice in the lower abdomen – thus earning himself the Iron Cross Second Class, First Class and Knight's Cross all within the space of a few days. Kepplinger and his comrades wear the distinctive camouflage smock and helmet cover worn by SS troops, with the SS insignia (apart from the patches on the exposed tunic collars) concealed. Kepplinger was also given a battlefield commission to the rank of SS-Untersturmführer in recognition of his courage, and was the subject of a widely circulated propaganda postcard by Wolfgang Willrich, showing him in full camouflage combat kit. These postcards of Kepplinger are now prized collectors' items.

E: BOMBER PILOT WERNER BAUMBACH, THE SCOURGE OF ALLIED SHIPPING

Oberleutnant Werner Baumbach is shown here with two NCOs from his crew (Baumbach is the middle figure) in front of his Junkers Ju 88 bomber, the aircraft in which he made his reputation and earned his Knight's Cross. The Ju 88 was an excellent medium bomber with dive-bombing capabilities. Its twin Jumo 211 engines gave it a top speed of over 500kph. With a crew of four, the A-4 version flown by Baumbach had a defensive armament of five 7.92mm machine guns and carried an offensive payload of up to 2,500kg of bombs. The dive-bombing capabilities of the Ju 88 meant that it could often escape from faster enemy fighters by going into a steep dive. An aircraft with these capabilities in the hands of an expert flier such as Baumbach made an awesome weapon. Many of the great Luftwaffe fighter aces were known as superb marksmen, but few bomber aces attracted the same plaudits. Baumbach used his skills to great effect in the precision bombing of enemy shipping, and in the course of his career he sank a larger tonnage of enemy shipping than even the great U-boat aces. His expertise as a flier was matched by his strength of character. Baumbach had several confrontations with the Luftwaffe hierarchy, always speaking his mind, often quite bluntly and without regard for the consequences. Despite this tendency to confront bureaucratic incompetence at higher levels, he continued his distinguished military career through to the end of the war, and was regarded as a highly respected bomber 'expert'.

F: SS-UNTERSTURMFÜHRER FRITZ VOGT CAPTURES AN ENEMY COLUMN, FRANCE 1940

Fritz Vogt is shown here with members of his motorcycle recce troop, who have intercepted a large column of enemy vehicles attempting to flee the rapid German advance. The resultant capture of the vehicles, 250 prisoners and two artillery pieces contributed to the award of his Knight's Cross. By this time Vogt had taken part in over 20 successful combat recce missions during the French campaign and was typical of the extremely keen and aggressive young officer class. Vogt's first major action during the campaign in the West had resulted in a major enemy bunker system being seized and over 200 enemy prisoners taken for the loss of just two of his own men and a few others lightly wounded. His second action was even more successful, with an enemy column being overrun and 650 prisoners taken, with only 30 of his own troops involved. Vogt is shown here in officer's field uniform, with an Army-style square belt, partially rolled-up camouflage smock and puttees instead of leather boots, and he is armed with an MP38 machine pistol. Vogt went on to serve with consistent élan throughout the remainder of the war, often involved in bitter hand-to-hand fighting. He was mortally wounded in March 1945, and was awarded the Oak-Leaves for his Knight's Cross just before he died.

G: MAJOR LUDWIG STAUTNER IN THE BATTLE FOR NARVIK, NORWAY 1940

The battle for Narvik was a close-run thing. On the naval side it was a disaster, with the bulk of the German destroyer fleet lost in action with the Royal Navy. On land, Ludwig Stautner's battalion of Gebirgsjäger (mountain troops) from Regiment 139 hung on tenaciously under considerable pressure from the Allied units that surrounded them. The German perimeter was gradually reduced, so much so that General Dietl was forced to consider the prospect of defeat and capture: the Allies had even landed and retaken the town of Narvik itself. However, the Germans put up a steadfast defence of the rapidly shrinking perimeter, and the Allies decided to pull back from the town: both Dietl and Stautner's mountain troops were the heroes of the hour. Dietl himself commented, however: 'They call me the Hero of Narvik, but if the battle had lasted one more day, I would have surrendered.' For his part in the dogged defence, Stautner was awarded the Knight's Cross.

Stautner is shown wearing the standard Army field blouse, but his Gebirgsjäger status is marked by the Edelweiss badge on his right sleeve, his mountain trousers, puttees, heavily cleated mountain boots and mountain cap. Stautner also wears the Heeresbergführer badge on his lower right chest indicating his status as an expert mountaineer. This rare award was bestowed only on the most skilled mountaineers, and was not dependent on rank or status. He is armed with an MP38 machine pistol.

H: OBERLEUTNANT RUDOLF WITZIG IN THE ASSAULT ON EBEN EMAEL, 10 MAY 1940

Rudolf Witzig is shown leading his parachute assault squad, codenamed 'Section Granite', in the attack on the Belgian fortress at Eben Emael, for which he earned the Knight's Cross. Witzig was one of the rare examples of a soldier being decorated with the Iron Cross Second Class, First Class and Knight's Cross all on the same day. Due to problems with his glider, Witzig arrived at Eben Emael several hours after his men, who had made good progress in his absence but were now meeting stiff resistance. His arrival encouraged his men to rally and launch a determined attack, which finally routed the defenders. His achievement in capturing a heavily defended key enemy position along with 1,200 prisoners, using only 85 men and suffering only six casualties, certainly warranted the Knight's Cross distinction. Witzig was also promoted to Hauptmann.

Witzig is wearing the so-called 'bone-sack', a one-piece step-in parachutist's smock: the early style worn here was in plain field grey, while later versions were cut from camouflage materials. He also wears the rimless helmet worn only by Fallschirmjäger, notably covered with a rough finish camouflage (achieved by mixing mud and earth with paint) and paratrooper jump boots. He is armed with the MP38 machine pistol, favoured by the Fallschirmjäger officer and NCO ranks prior to the introduction of their own paratrooper rifle.

INDEX